BOW HUNTING
FOR BIG GAME

BOW HUNTING FOR BIG GAME

Keith C. Schuyler

Stackpole Books

BOW HUNTING FOR BIG GAME

Copyright © 1974 by
Keith C. Schuyler

Published by
STACKPOLE BOOKS
Cameron and Kelker Streets
Harrisburg, Pa. 17105

Printed in the U.S.A.

Library of Congress Cataloging in Publication Data

Schuyler, Keith C
    Bow hunting for big game.

      1. Hunting with bow and arrow— North America. 2. Big game hunting—
North America. 3. Hunting with bow and arrow—Law and legislation—North
America.
I. Title.
SK36.S38   799.2'15   74-6276
ISBN 0-8117-0309-6

To my last arrow—
neither is certain
where the other shall fall

Other Books by the Author

LURES—The Guide to Sport Fishing

ELUSIVE HORIZONS

ARCHERY—From Golds to Big Game

Unless otherwise noted, all photos were taken or provided by the author.

Contents

Foreword

This may be the first book written on advanced bow hunting with the gun hunter in mind. Occasional references to gunning at least allude to the fact that information and procedures which are successful in the more demanding sport of bow hunting will most certainly work in gun hunting. And, today many hunters alternate with both arms in their pursuit of big game.

The writer has had considerable experience with each although the bow has become his favored arm. He recognizes that no one can have all the answers. Nevertheless, this work covers the most important questions. It is particularly directed to those sportsmen who may wish to vary their local hunting with trips far afield for other species of big game.

The appendix, which covers all the United States and Canadian provinces, provides a base from which to plan a trip far afield. Many chapters expand upon it. But, those who may never leave their familiar hunting areas can take vicarious enjoyment in breathing the thin air of sheep country or listening to the freight-train charge of a bull moose through a thicket or dodging the spray of an enraged Atlantic stingray.

This is a sport that, because of the need for close approach to game, entails certain hazards to the hunter. Whether a case of *possible* mistaken identity by a huge bear that challenged the author, a probable charge by a wounded mule deer buck, or a sticky battle with a big hammerhead shark, bow hunting hasn't changed greatly since its inception many thousands of years ago.

Although the chapters on each species of big game primarily cover ways to find and get shooting, earlier sections deal with basic tackle and methods. In total, this book is a practical approach to bow hunting in your favorite haunts, the more remote mountains and forests, barren northern wastes, prairie country, and even on the volcanic slopes of our newest state, Hawaii.

Those steeped in bow hunting, or gun hunting, will be prepared for the text's rapid, yet meticulous pace concerning pursuit of the various big game species with the bow and arrow. Others, who have not yet mastered the elementary skills of archery, will find encouragement to improve both their knowledge and abilities.

This is a hunting sportsman's book. It is written by one who claims the right to kill in the *name* of sport. But, this right is always subjugated to the needs of the ecosystem and the perpetuation of hunting as a sport.

It is the newest approach to one of the oldest contests in the world—bow hunting for big game. It is a sport in which the element of risk sometimes restores a dimension that is not for the fainthearted.

Preface

There are three very real and vital reasons for this book from the writer's view. Having been intimately associated with archers and archery for much of the past thirty-five years, my thoughts have been tempered by time and the times. Although I have followed the tournament circuit, and tasted the mild wine of modest victory, when the competition wasn't too tough, it was the love of hunting that brought me into archery and that has kept me there.

So, the primary reason for what follows is simply to offer what I have learned and experienced so that the reader might sort out what he can best use. As I always told my three sons, you should step well out ahead of me because you will have your own knowledge and experiences to build upon what I share with you.

Secondly, it is the gun hunter who is by far in the majority today among bow hunters. Too much is written for the target archer who goes bow hunting without regard for the rifleman who has been attracted to archery in his hunting sport. Actually, the number of hunters today who use *only the bow* is a small fraction of the total in bow hunting. Most started with the gun and have picked up the bow for the extra days *of* hunting as well as the extra sport *in* hunting. This book is written primarily for them but also for those who are just now being tempted by the challenge and the opportunity.

The third reason for this writing is almost paradoxical. It is to encourage more hunting in a space of history when each year there is less land on which to hunt. Part of this shrinkage is simple mathematics. Each increase in the number of hunters reduces the individual area to hunt. Another cause of shrinkage is the annual increase in the number of trespass notices because of the pressure generated by increasing numbers of hunters. A more ominous cause is the extension of rural housing which leads to laws prohibiting the use of flat-shooting, high-powered guns. The bow can and, already in some more heavily populated areas, is filling the void. Although the ancient hunting sport's rebirth in recent years at first met considerable opposition from the gun-toting fraternity, literally hundreds of thousands of riflemen are now archers in season.

But, to preserve the very implication of sport-seeking in use of the bow, we must be good hunters and good sportsmen. The following chapters I trust will be of help in hunting all species of big game with the bow and arrow. Sportsmanship is an individual proposition in which each hunter will be best judged by his own conscience.

So that the reader might have a further clue as to the person responsible for the chapters that follow, some of his inner thoughts stand naked in these verses.

A Target Of My Mind

What drives me drives the shaft
That seeks a life expendable
For those who study at their craft.

I seek the thrill and not the kill
That crowns a shot commendable,
That joined my thought with my own skill.

My practiced hand and studied eye
Are yet not proof dependable,
But less than this the gods decry.

For me there is no compromise,
Less than my best deserves no prize;
And if my best brings but a miss,
I thank God just for all of this.

Keith C. Schuyler.

CHAPTER 1

The Name of the Game

When you talk to an old hunter, especially if his inner thoughts are pried loose by fruit of the vine, or he just gets in a sentimental mood, you discover one of the best known secrets of the fraternity. He may even be almost apologetic about it. And, his age as a hunter is counted in years spent at the sport rather than his total chronological accumulation. But, what happens to him is a little victory of our so-called civilization. He will admit to it, often with a puzzled shake of his head, softly.

"The killin' has kind of gotten to me."

At first glance, some might think that this is a hell of a way to start off a book on hunting!

The thought hit me about sixteen years ago when my oldest son was approaching his twelfth birthday. I had taken my share of game; there was nothing left to prove. But, I didn't want my sons to miss the experience. On the other hand, I didn't want to enforce my pleasures on them. Each took an interest in varying degrees. Bringing them along the trails to find the love of hunting and the hunted, the special kind of affection that develops for bows and guns and dogs and scents and signs

13

of it all, renewed the old man's interest. Just seeing the youngsters develop replaced the compelling enthusiasm and excitement that my dad had engendered in me.

I didn't stop shooting although more and more I carried the bow. But, the most important shots now came from either side of me, or down in the woods on a drive.

However, long before my youngsters were born, when I was a very young man myself, archery as a means to the hunting sport had taken hold of me. I made my first bow and killed my first arrow-shot deer with it. For years it was more of a novelty than a serious way of hunting until I had taken my share of game and dissipated the feverish desire to shoot whatever the law allowed.

For the same reason that the angler limits himself to artificial lures; for the same reason that the muzzleloader limits himself to an archaic weapon; for the same reason some hunters shoot only a pistol —I turned more and more to the bow. It presented a greater challenge.

Who said it first is immaterial, but countless hunters today agree that it is a bigger thrill to miss a deer with a bow than it is to kill one with a gun. An exception is that first deer, the most likely big game for all hunters. Nothing can take away the thrill of the first success no matter what the circumstances.

But, each success with the bow becomes a special event. The

Hunting big game with the bow is the greater challenge.

normally exciting anticipation, with the quarry within sight from moments to many minutes before the shot, is something that must be experienced to be appreciated. And then, at that instant when you must put it all together, when you must depend upon your own muscles and a primitive weapon, when every twig, the very air, the animal's instinct, and everything that you have suddenly forgotten, contrive against you, you release. And the arrow must cut through your misgivings and all these other obstacles to reach the quarry, or a leaf, or a limb, a log. No matter what it hits, the experience leaves you emotionally drawn and physically drained. Unless, in the rare instance, you get a second try before your adrenalin has completed its wrecking job.

It is an awesome thing to release an arrow at a living creature when it is within the usual shooting range. Like hand to hand combat, it becomes a much more personal thing. You are much more emotionally a part of the shot than at the usual gun range. It is a part of you.

It has been said that the only truly wild instinct left to a domestic cow is that which compels her to hide and occasionally defend her newborn calf. Otherwise, she is almost completely dependent upon man. To a degree, man has become almost as subservient to civilization.

The one wild instinct which developed out of his need, and which is retained, is that which makes him lord over the lower animals—food getting. The need is no longer there for educated and civilization softened homo sapiens, but the instinct remains. It *will* find an outlet. Seeking wild creatures, not for food as a necessity, but for the pure love of the hunt, is what attracts man to the sport. And, if he does not expend his basic savagery in a controlled environment, he may find other ways to do so. How often have those who resist modern society in the name of peace resorted to violence against their fellow man?

It must be admitted that there is a very small minority among us who never do rise above the basic instinct to kill. These relative few will never understand what is being attempted in these paragraphs. There are young hunters as eager as I who will maybe wonder and perhaps fear the possibility that their initial enthusiasm might some day be dampened if the killing gets to them. If so, they might be fortified by a look around them to count men several times their age who still enjoy the chase as much as ever—but, who have never *enjoyed* the killing.

Hunting is killing. The death of some creature marks the culmination of the chase, the sport. It is unavoidable no matter how we might try to gloss over it. But, it is significant that the trophy, if it is retained, is restored as much as possible to how it looked in life. Its beauty and grandeur is retained many times over its normal life span.

Mounts preserve the grandeur of creatures many times their normal life span.

I find no grounds to deny man his right to take the life of a lower animal. The only counter argument with any substance must come from a confirmed vegetarian. But, even he or she, if a Christian or a Jew, must find an argument outside the realm of religion to debate the subject. Christ didn't hesitate to transfer a set of demons in Job to a herd of pigs which promptly drowned in a nearby lake (Luke 8-33; Matthew 8-32; Mark 5-13). St. Mark estimated the herd at about two thousand. Drop back to the first twelve chapters of Leviticus to discover that countless animals were offered as somewhat grisly sacrifices.

And yet, I cannot hold with such as Roger Caras who states in his book, *Death As a Way of Life*, (Little, Brown and Company), "As killers we were born and as killers we live." He presents his *opinion* as an accomplished fact by posing the question, "Is it any wonder that man *loves* to kill?"

I personally find nothing in the history of man that even hints of a universal love of killing. Rather, it is the contest, whether between man and man or man and beast. Even the American Indian paid homage to the game he killed.

A rebuttal might point up the fact that the hunter should seem to be able to satisfy his competitive desires by shooting trap or skeet. Let's face it. Some of the shots from a mechanical trap are far more challenging than the average wing shot in the field. But, the shooter stands on the line in the knowledge that the clay bird will be released at his command by another human within a certain known area. It cannot even closely compare to the thrill of an unexpected flush of grouse from under foot or a tangle of wild grape vines.

We can take our subject one step further. Fishermen kill fish; some even let them flop their lives out in a creel. Yet, there has never been a hue and cry against fishermen as killers. Commercial fishermen dump thousands of live fish into a ship's hold where they suffocate to death. Yes, a fish is an impersonal, cold-blooded being somewhat further removed from man than a warm-blooded animal, but it is a living creature. Nevertheless, there is a type of fisherman, that includes me, who quickly dispatch a fish intended for the pan or tenderly release one that is being returned to the water.

If the foregoing is interpreted as a defense of hunting, it is not intended to be. Rather, it is intended as an explanation of why man continues to hunt in this day when the need for food gathering is no longer a valid reason for those who can afford hunting equipment. If all he wanted to do was kill, he could just as easily afford to buy some animals and birds to indulge this desire.

When bow hunting was revived as a popular sport after World War II, it was gun hunters who resisted the most. Of course, some did so because they considered archers as intruders into the hunting sport despite the fact that the bow predated the gun by many thousands of years. But, the vast majority, according to personal association and perusal of detracting articles written early on the subject, objected because they thought the arrow to be a cruel way to kill.

As more and more states recognized bow hunting and offered special concessions for this limited means of pursuit, it became evident that

In bow hunting, it is the contest that counts.

gun hunters were adopting the attitude of, "If you can't beat 'em; join 'em." Although it is difficult to prove this on a man to man basis, Pennsylvania statistics offer incontrovertible evidence. The number in organized archery as represented by the Pennsylvania State Archery Association and its affiliated clubs remained fairly stable at around 3,000 over a considerable span of years. Yet, from a low of 5,542 in the first buck-only archery season held in the state in 1951, the number of those purchasing the special archery tag rose to about 148,000 in the first twenty years. In its first year of existence, Pennsylvania Bow Hunters Association attracted some 3,000 members without a visible program!

The frequent use here of Pennsylvania as a basis for certain truths about bow hunting has more substance than in the simple fact that this writer was born and raised in the Keystone State. Its Game Commission keeps a close tab on bow hunting activities through the licensing procedure, which reveals the number of participants, and kill reports, which make it possible to keep track of the harvest.

While regulated seasons and concentration of all types of hunters does amount to a substantial harvest of wild creatures in the name of sport, this is only part of the picture. Those who oppose the vast army of outdoor sportsmen should look elsewhere to validate their claims of cruelty.

Let them start with Nature herself. Every twenty-four hours of the day there is enacted a thousand times a thousand times the killing that is part of a healthy ecosystem. And, wild creatures are not regulated. A wolf will hamstring a caribou and start feeding before the animal is dead. Domestic dogs, friendly pets of the living room, can, and actually do attack deer if they are permitted to roam in winter. Wildcats feed heavily on other creatures. House cats, permitted to run freely or become feral, do the same.

It is only because encroaching civilization has removed most predators that man's hand is actually *needed* to maintain a balance between certain animals and birds and the food available to them. The alternatives of disease and starvation, Nature's emergency controls, are the most cruel of all. Either man or wild creatures must be permitted to dominate. A moot choice, perhaps, but nevertheless, it is a truism.

Little is said by alarmists about one of our worst killers and maimers, the highway vehicle. In 1972, vehicles alone killed—by actual count—26,435 whitetailed deer on Pennsylvania highways. It is fair to estimate that an additional ten percent staggered off into the woods to die a far worse death than that imposed by the average bullet or arrow.

A studied example of the results that archers produce when bow hunting for deer has been obtained from Missouri's Knob Noster State Park. After 1,000 hunters participated in a hunt in 1960 and tagged 136 deer, a post-hunt search was made under the direction of the Department of Conservation and only three *dead* deer were found that had not been recovered. In 1969, after a hunt produced 416 archers who claimed 40 deer, only one unrecovered deer was found. The following year, 426 hunters took 37 deer and no dead ones were found. In 1972, only one unrecovered deer was found after a hunt by 539 archers. (A hunt was also held in 1971 but no search was made.) It is significant that *no wounded deer* were found in any of the post-hunting searches.

In this day of do-gooders and uninformed sentimentalists, all hunters must be alert to protect the out-of-doors that they have largely preserved and paid for through license fees and taxes. Certain members of the general news media—the press, the radio, the television—seem quick to further anything derogatory to guns or to hunting, evidently preferring instead to foster the Bambi concept.

Vehicles killed, by actual count, 26,435 deer in one year in Pennsylvania.

Somehow a certain segment of the public has forgotten or refuses to accept the fact that man's ancestors ate wild game with their fingers, killing the game with no concern as to how it died. It is just a matter of geography as to where the white man made his gory way, where the Indian ate off the land, and where some societies still continue to do so. When the red man chased moose into the water off Maine's Mount Desert Island or drove bison off the canyon cliffs of Wyoming, he did so as a matter of survival. He shot the swimming moose with bows and speared the broken buffalo so that he could eat. Conservation then was unnecessary and unknown for the most part. But today, the hunter has set for himself rules of conservation and sportsmanship so that wild creatures can be both enjoyed and preserved in numbers consistent with habitat and available food.

Guns have been under attack from many quarters because people have done some bad things with them. People have also done some bad things with rocks, golf clubs, tire irons, knives and clubs. But, since guns have serial numbers, some politicians feel that they can be registered, restricted, or confiscated. Some formerly important politicians are no longer important because they advocated one or several actions against guns. All outdoor people must stick together to preserve in fact and by law the rights of wild creatures and sensible men. Archers and gunners, who frequently wear the same hat, have a dual stake in outdoor America.

It should also be considered that archers can seldom harvest enough animals even where overproduction of game threatens its own existence. Such areas also usually need a gunning season from time to time to help maintain a proper balance in game population.

This business of law in hunting is an extremely serious part of the game. Those who wink at the law or consider it okay for the other fellow but not for themselves are the worst enemies of those who love the sport of hunting. They are not sportsmen in any sense if they take unto themselves advantages denied the law-abiding hunters. They would be thrown out of the game in any other sport, and hunting should offer no exception. It is the duty of those who do play by the rules to report the infractions of those who don't. This still holds true even though it becomes a thin line sometimes when one is hunting outside his state of residence where the rules may differ from those of his own state. But the officials who make the rules don't provide exceptions for those who happen to come from some other ball park.

There is one other fellow who is endangering future hunting who plays by all the rules except one. He may be a great companion, an excellent hunter, and a true sportsman in his approach to his game. However, he cannot resist the temptation to take more for himself than the law allows. In so doing, he is stealing from his fellow sportsmen. He would be shocked to find his name on a list of "game hogs," but he writes his own tag.

Aside from his offense to the sport and his fellow sportsmen, there is another and increasingly obvious penalty from the law breaker's behavior. We are losing hunting land by accumulative masses each year. Even with a 150-yard safety zone around each occupied building, every new rural home or the mobile home mounted on cinder blocks at the edge of some wood lot takes away 14.6 acres of land from hunting.

The Economic Research Service estimates that about 34 million acres of land, much of it wildlife habitat, will disappear by the year

Each rural home takes away over 14 acres of land from hunting.

2000. Rural land areas are being taken at the rate of 750,000 acres annually by urban growth; roads and airports have taken another 130,000; and reservoirs remove about 300,000 a year. If this rate of loss continues, 34 million acres will take from hunting an area 500 miles long and 100 miles wide. This area is even larger than that of some of the smaller states.

This is normal "growth". But, each year many thousands more acres are closed to public hunting by landowners who have been offended by careless or malicious hunters. It only takes a few stupid people to ruin it for the vast majority. Sportsmen have a stake and a responsibility to stamp out the "stupids" by turning them in to the proper officials.

Over a period of many years, I have made personal efforts to learn the effects of an arrow on living flesh. Since deer aren't talking, I have interviewed a number of persons who have been from mildly to severely wounded by arrows. In each instance, *initial* pain was negligible if it was felt at all. Mental trauma associated with such events is much more painful because of the implications relative to possible loss of life, loss of employment, cost of medical bills, etc. An animal does not suffer these concerns.

The most startling example of an arrow mishap with which I am closely familiar happened to a hunting acquaintance in New Mexico. Donald Dvoroznak was standing on a snow-covered rock one day in January, 1972, when he twisted to draw on a deer. He slipped, and somehow the arrow jabbed into him as he fell. The broadhead, which fortunately had lost the razor-edge insert, entered his chest between the seventh and eighth rib and penetrated upward to nick the bottom of his right lung. He packed the wound with snow and walked about a mile and a half before finding assistance. A short time after he left the hospital, where he had spent five days, I couldn't resist adding to my notes on the general subject of physiological reaction to arrow wounds.

"All I felt was a bump," Don said. "In fact, I didn't even know the arrow was in me until I saw blood on the broken shaft."

The arrow had an aluminum shaft. Anyone familiar with the resiliency of this tubular metal can appreciate the force necessary to break it. Don had an extremely close call.

Most readers have probably had the experience of cutting themselves without realizing it until they saw blood. This is not to discount the pain later associated with such wounds, but it is rare that much physical pain is felt at the moment of the mishap.

Reports from those who have survived bullet wounds have been similar. Either there was no realization that they had been shot or the sensation was that of a bump.

Of course, the mentioned facts must be taken only as generalizations. Initial pain, or the span of time before pain does occur, will be determined somewhat by nerve involvement.

Consequently, it is a fair assumption that an animal *usually* feels little or no pain upon being hit by either a bullet or an arrow. In most instances, the animal will take off for the nearest exit at a dead run if it has not been bowled over by the shot. However, this is more likely because of the noise and/or movement of the hunter which the animal somehow associates with the attack on its anatomy. For, there have been many instances with the bow and some with the gun, where the animal was mortally wounded and seemed unaware that it had a problem. It either stood in some apparent confusion, or walked around until it suddenly fell over dead.

It must be kept in mind that the normal reaction of any wild animal that realizes it is in danger, is to run as fast as it can to a position of relative security. As soon as this position is reached, the animal will stop to reassess the situation. If it feels secure, it will stand a while if unhurt, and then resume feeding or the search for feed. If mortally wounded, it will lie down simply because instinct tells it to do so. This is the same instinct which caused it to rush headlong across the meadow or into the bush when first alarmed.

How far it will go depends, of course, upon the individual animal or the species, and how alarmed it has become.

This points up the need for a clean kill. From both the humane and practical standpoints, it is desirable to place the arrow as well as possible into a vital area. If the game is to be taken, the kill is the necessary culmination of the hunt. The end result, nevertheless, does not preclude compassion as a proper companion accompanying the hunter to the most remote part of the forest. I make no excuse for the kill. But, since it does remove a living creature from Nature's store, I accept the personal responsibility of doing it with as much efficiency and dispatch as I can command.

There are three requirements for a good hunt with the bow. One has to do with fitting proper equipment to the archer. The second is the need to adapt or acquire the special hunting skills necessary to some consistency of success with the bow. And the last is the ability to score cleanly at distances within the archer's skill zone.

We are going to take a look at each of these areas with the hope that the reader might better his chances. There is probably less guarantee of success in bow hunting, however, than any other sport which comes to mind. Oh, we can all talk about the wonderful time available, whether or not a score is made. But, everyone must win once in a while so that he doesn't forget the name of the game. It is: Bow Hunting for Big Game.

CHAPTER 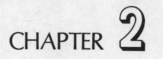 2

The Bow, The Arrow and You

Since the purpose here is to set the scene for a good bow hunt and follow-through, the assumption is that the reader is a hunter. However, ability to score on game with the gun or to rip the gold out of a target with the bow are not sufficient qualifications for bow hunting.

This may come as a surprise. Gunners probably figure that a good target archer should be a good bow hunter. And, it would seem that a hunter who has been successful with the gun for many years shouldn't find it too difficult to switch to the bow. Well, it just isn't necessarily so in either case.

Some answers to why it frequently isn't so can be explained. Some reasons can only be suspected. But, it is a many-times proven fact that excellent target archers sometimes fail miserably on the hunting scene. I am not going to name names, but I have personally known champion archers to look hard and long for their first deer kill. It was not their inability to get close to game, either. They simply missed! And, many times these misses came at distances where they ordinarily could literally place six arrows in a row, time after time, within a three-inch circle.

Some archers practice well with the best in equipment.

These archers take to the field with the very best in tackle. They have practiced well; they are completely familiar with their equipment; they are good hunters. Yet, something happens at that moment when everything must come together. They miss.

It should be understood, however, that some of the very best bow hunters are also expert target archers. In fact, the bowman who perfects his style on the target line, retains his knowledge and ability in the field, and is also a good hunter, is most likely to score and to continue to score on big game. Those of lesser accuracy with the bow may make up in hunting skill what they lack in shooting ability. They must get closer to the target.

Then, coming in on the other side of the wood lot is the fellow who has hunted with the gun for many years and figures it should be fairly easy to dump a deer with the bow. After all, he has many times seen does within a fly rod's length during buck season, and sometimes vice versa. He can't see wasting all that time shooting at bull's-eyes. Hell, if he can hit a stump or a tin can in the back yard, it should be easy to hit anything as big as a deer!

Well, it should be. But it isn't. Especially it isn't with the tackle carried by the average first-time bow hunter, the one who can't stand those creeps down at the archery club. Anyone who can shoot a gun can pick up any gun that doesn't have its sights knocked crooked, and do a fair job. It doesn't hold true with the bow and arrow. It never did; and it never will.

Before we go any further into this subject, we'd better take a look at the exceptions. The young kid, the girl, the first-time-out gun hunter, none of whom should have a chance, sometimes make all studied judgments look silly. They borrow a bow and arrows, or pick up some junk at a discount house, take a couple hours off from their regular duties, and come home a hero, or a heroine. Somehow, circumstances contrive to make everything come out just right when all the odds scream that it can't be done. These crazy facts of fate provide the unknown quantities which make poker players edgy when a woman or a complete novice takes a hand.

We're just going to ignore them while they go eat venison or win the state lottery or sink an oil well with a fence post. Meanwhile, there is this serious side to bow hunting.

First things come first. In bow hunting, tackle—that equipment which is directly concerned with getting the arrowhead into the vital area of an animal—should always be considered first. Since there is so much excellent tackle available today, only generalizations will be presented here. This is not because of reticence to mention brand names per se, it is just that competition among bow manufacturers changes the edge from year to year relative to quality. But, like blue-chip stocks, certain better known brands usually collect at the top because they have earned it by past performance.

Any recurve bow of sufficient drawing weight, with wood and fiberglass laminations, that sells around fifty dollars or above, should be able to deliver an arrow sufficiently well to take any of the big game species. But, this is only the starting point. The bow must fit the need. Further, the arrow must fit the bow. And both must fit the hunter.

Somewhere along the line, because sufficient cast could be built into the excellent bows available today, there was a push toward short bows. They have a few, very few, advantages. It is easier to shoot a short bow from a tree stand since the lower limb will clear your perch easier than a longer bow. It is a bit easier to handle in thick brush for the rare shot when you are frozen into position by the appearance of the quarry and have minimum clearance to draw. It is a bit lighter to carry at the end of a long day's hunt. That's about it.

On the negative side, one disadvantage rules them out for me. They are more difficult to shoot. Being lighter in mass weight, they don't provide the stability needed for the bow arm. The angle of the string tends to pinch the fingers of the drawing hand together. All that power being constricted into a shorter frame tends to produce the equivalent of kick in a light gun. If short bows were better, you would see them on the tournament shooting line. But you don't.

Since bows are normally carried in a horizontal position except for the shot, longer bows will clear the brush as well or better than the shorter offerings. As to any advantage shorter bows might have in air or motor transit, modern take-down bows eliminate any such edge.

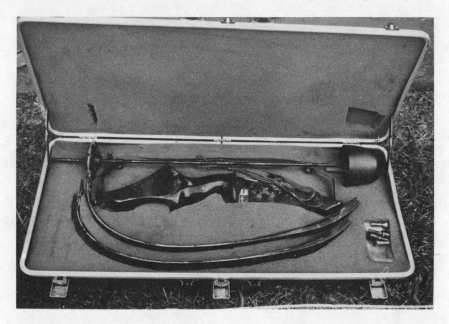

Takedown bows, such as this Wing, easily cased, eliminate any length advantage.

So, if you are looking for your first bow or are thinking of a swap, at least try out a bow of no less than sixty inches before you make a final decision.

Next, for a hunting bow, follow the trend taken particularly by so-called bare-bow target archers. Get a bow just as heavy as you can comfortably handle. The field-target archer shoots all he can handle because it reduces the trajectory of the arrow and lessens the compensation he must make when aiming at the target. A heavier bow for hunting has the same advantage and a couple more for good measure.

Reduction of trajectory will give you an edge when shooting through brush. Your arrow is less apt to pick up a stray twig, leaf, or limb along the way to steer it off target. Greater power will give your arrow greater penetration.

Game laws which take bow weight into consideration seldom permit less than a forty-pound bow. Of course, this doesn't mean a blessed thing any more than the laws which state that a bow must be capable of casting an arrow so many yards. If the archer doesn't draw his arrow sufficiently far on the string when shooting at game, he can be getting well under forty pounds on a seventy-pound bow. And, his arrow may be incapable of reaching the legal distance even if the bow is held at a forty-five degree angle for the shot.

Consequently, it is most important that a bow hunter buy a bow of a weight which he can comfortably handle and hold at *full draw* for at least the time needed to take careful aim. This should normally be about five seconds. However, if the animal is moving, it may be necessary to hold at partial or full draw for considerably longer. But, as a studied generalization, he should be able to hold without quivering for the full five seconds. At full draw.

Okay, what's full draw?

With a broadhead on the arrow, full draw is roughly when the back of the head is within one-quarter of an inch from the riser, or the handle section, of the bow. Technically, it is when the base of the arrowhead sleeve meets the back of the riser. It should not be against the bow since this may tend to throw the arrow off line at the release. Clickers are made which can be set to release at the exact draw length. However, they are just another distraction and a possible means of alerting the game we have tried so hard to deceive. It is better, in my opinion, to practice until full draw is second nature and can be accomplished almost unconsciously. And, the only way to make this come about is to establish your proper draw and have arrows made to fit. The only way to determine that your arrows will fit is to first establish an anchor.

An anchor, and it must be constant, is that point at which your draw fingers touch some part of your face. You must shoot many arrows to find an anchor that is comfortable. The closer this is to your shooting eye, the easier it is to compensate for the distance between the visual point of your arrow and the spot on the animal you wish to hit. My personal anchor is such that my forefinger lightly touches the bottom edge of my right nostril. If I don't hold exactly at that spot on my face, my arrow doesn't have a chance because all my visual and mental compensations are geared to that pressure against my face and the touch of my nose.

And, that arrow must be at full draw.

That means that the distance from the throat of the nock on the bow string to where the broadhead just clears the back of my bow must

Fred Paden, using compound bow, illustrates full draw.

always be the same. And, that distance is *my* draw length. It is obtained by extending my bow arm to its full length and drawing until my fingers are anchored at the same spot.

This, of course, is how you determine what length arrow you need. For the average archer, this distance will be about twenty-eight inches. Some archery shops have a scaled arrow that you can draw so that your length can be read from it at full draw. Don't settle for arrows longer or shorter than *your* proper draw length.

That's not quite all. The arrows must be spined for your draw length as it relates to the weight of your bow. Bows are normally weighed at twenty-eight inches. That is, a fifty-pound bow will draw an arrow of that length until the back edge of the head meets the back of the bow when a weight of fifty pounds is applied to the string. If your draw is more or less than twenty-eight inches, *your* bow becomes either lighter or heavier. To determine how much per inch, divide the factory-marked weight by twenty. For example, twenty goes into fifty, two and one-half times. If you draw your fifty-pound bow but twenty-seven inches, it is a forty-seven and one-half pound bow when you are using it. If you draw twenty-nine inches, your fifty-pound bow is actually fifty-two and one-half pounds. This is only an approximation, but it will be close. Better yet, have your bow weighed at your draw on a machine (see photo). Factory stamped weights are not always accurate.

Your arrows should normally be spined for *your* draw weight rather than the factory weight marked on the bow. Occasionally, because of some peculiar physical characteristic, you may require a spine a bit different than that recommended for your draw weight. It is well to practice with a couple arrow spines on either side of that recommended by the manufacturer's chart if you have trouble.

Spine is the property of the arrow shaft to resist bending. Since it is desirable that the arrow bend to some degree so that it may absorb the side pressure as it passes the sight window of the bow, this varies according to the weight bow and the length of shaft. With aluminum, this can be determined precisely and nearly so with fiberglass because the bending properties can be predetermined to a fine degree. With wood, this amount of deflection from center is determined by attaching a two-pound weight at the center of the shaft with the shaft supported at two places twenty-six inches apart.

The only advantage that wood has is its generally lower price. I personally do not favor wood because of its splintering qualities which can turn a superficial hit into a painful wound. Without going further into the potential traumatic qualities of wood, which I have thoroughly explored, consider only the effects produced by a splinter in your own finger.

A bow-weighing machine will show weights at each draw, inch by inch.

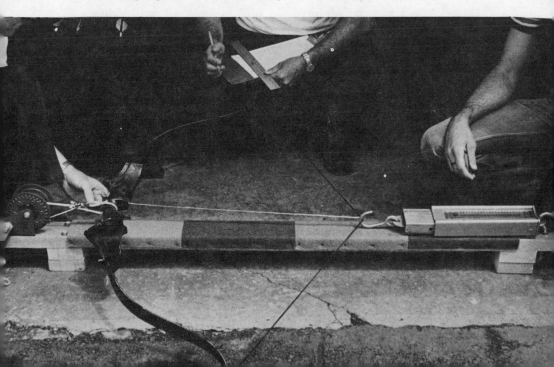

Although aluminum shafts can be made somewhat more precisely, there is room for argument in a comparison of this metal with fiberglass. Lighter weight of aluminum permits a greater speed and consequently a somewhat flatter trajectory. Fiberglass has a potentially greater penetrating ability because of its heavier weight for a given spine. Whether there is sufficient difference to favor one over the other for either reason is a moot question. Both make excellent hunting arrow shafts. Aluminum is a bit more expensive.

Choice of broadheads is not nearly so important as the ability to place them properly into the animal. However, claims of bone-breaking or bone penetrating ability are negatives on my chart. Rather, the capability of a head to cut cleanly, and to cut as much as possible, are the plus values I seek. Frankly, except for the ribs, which are fairly easy to cut through, I prefer that my arrowhead bounce off or slide past a bone. It will be a rare occasion when breaking or shooting through a major bone with an arrow will bring a big-game animal down within recovery distance of a bow hunter.

As long as an arrowhead will not plane in flight, and the greater area its cutting surfaces have, the more initial damage it will do. Four cutting edges are obviously better than three, and three better than two, if the total cutting surface when viewed horizontally is greater. And, it is important that the metal is such that it can be sharpened to a keen edge. An arrow must normally kill by hemorrhage. The more blood vessels it cuts, the quicker the animal will succumb to its wound. The cutting

Illustrating the wide selection of heads—one for each hunting purpose

edge must be sharp enough that it will sever tough veins and arteries rather than push them aside.

Extremely sharp points are not desirable. Rather, a point is more apt to do the damage intended if it will cause the head to slip off a bone into flesh rather than to stick in the bone or to bend over from contact with it.

One other factor relative to arrowheads is important to this writer from a humane standpoint. Barbed heads, or those which have trailing edges that prevent easy removal, can turn a superficial wound into a painful or a fatal one. It is a known fact that even a deer will frequently withdraw an arrow if the head is such that it can be withdrawn. Or, the arrow will work loose by itself. Consequently, if the trailing edge of the head is tapered to perhaps thirty degrees or more, it is less apt to cause much more than an annoyance in the event of a non-fatal hit.

This is an area that deserves more attention from the lawmakers than the impractical rules governing bow weights or the ability of the bow to cast an arrow so many yards. At least six states and two provinces have outlawed these barbed heads. All should.

Even the cutting edge, which is sometimes set by law at no less than seven-eighths to three-quarter inches minimum width, is much less important. Few bow hunters would be likely to buy arrowheads with less cutting area. Besides, a marginal head could be reduced in size from repeated sharpening to place the hunter in legal jeopardy where such minimums are set by law. Surely a *sharp* head of three-quarter inch is much preferred over a dull one half again as wide.

It is true that so-called tranquilizer, or poison heads are legal in some areas. The vast majority of states do not permit them nor do any provinces of Canada.

Because of the accent on safety and considerations of compassion for game threaded through this book, it might seem incongruous for this writer to take a stand against the apparent humane qualities of such hunting arrows. But, there have been far too many instances uncovered in my travels and research, wherein humans would have died to even remotely consider the use of such chemicals in hunting. In the quantities of succinylcholinechloride used in such arrows, it is pure poison.

Quite a number of hunters, some of whom are my close acquaintances, would today be dead if they had been using such chemicals. Further, human accidents would likely increase if this use became widespread. Certain idiots would be flinging arrows at anything that moved in any direction in the hope that the poison would finalize what they were unable to accomplish as hunters.

Again we are tempted into that gray area between hunting as a game and hunting as killing. The object is to approach close enough to the game animal to effect its demise with a clean shot. The game has already been won at the instant the point of the arrow separates the hair over a vital spot on the animal. The kill is anticlimactic. It is only a score and has nothing to do with the *sport* of hunting.

But, since there have been so many articles written, urging an open look at the "pod" arrow, let's attempt to be objective. Much of the writing has been pinned to Mississippi's favorable accident rate where the arrow was introduced by Dr. R. P. Herrington, its inventor, and an experimental hunt held in February, 1970. This hunt was arranged through the cooperation of the Mississippi Game and Fish Commission with the American Archery Council and Archery Manufacturers Organization.

On the hunt, a deer traveled 100 yards before succumbing to a shot with a pod arrow. The arrow passed completely through the flank. That is the area between the ribs and the hip, a poor hit although usually a fatal one. Mark down a plus for the pod.

However, in the thick foliage of early autumn in the Northeast, deer are sometimes lost that travel 100 yards if there is no good blood trail. It has been stated that a deer will become completely immobilized in 30 seconds after a good hit with the pod arrow. Although a white-tailed deer has been clocked up to 60 miles per hour, let's halve that and assume in rough terrain that it would travel only 30 miles per hour in its death flight. It *could* travel 440 yards, roughly one-quarter mile.

A look at the pod, containing succinylcholine chloride, as it is used on an arrow.

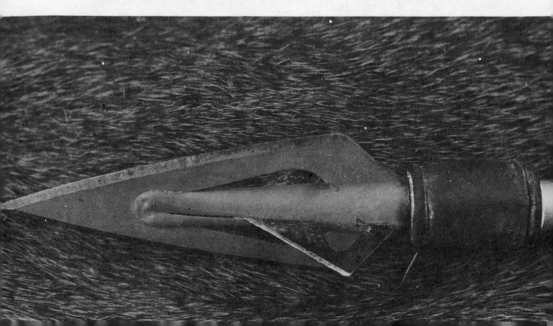

To cover much of the period when the pod arrow was permitted, not legalized, in Mississippi, take a look at the 1960 state statistics. Mississippi had a population density of but 45.1 people per square mile compared to Pennsylvania's 249.7. Mississippi had a total population of 2,178,141 compared to Pennsylvania's 11,319,366. The states offer a good comparison because they are quite close in size, 47,716 square miles for Mississippi, and the Keystone State has 45,333. Yet, in 1972, for example, Mississippi had 8,480 bow hunters to 160,759 licensed in Pennsylvania. In the same year, Mississippi reported 20 gun fatalities among 272,948 hunters to 19 in Pennsylvania among 1,100,000 gun hunters.

Pigmies and certain South American aborigines use poison on their arrowheads. But, their bows and arrows are so primitive that they need any advantage. It is their means of livelihood and protection.

It has been stated that the relatively few failures of the pod arrow have been involved in shoulder hits where there was insufficient penetration to get the proper effect from the poison. In two hard hits that I made, and exceedingly regret, wherein I thought there was a chance that the deer would succumb to the injury, both were in the shoulder.

Lord knows that I do not want to *hurt* any living creature although I have absolutely no compunctions about killing them in fair chase. But, I do not get overly excited about the loss of an animal that is fatally hit and is not recovered despite every reasonable hunter effort to find it. There are certain natural losses that contribute to the needs of other creatures that prey chiefly on deer, dead and alive. Highway kills in Pennsylvania exceeded 26,000 deer in 1972. Only a fraction of these animals were recovered for human consumption, and only a small percentage of the hides were saved for sale to replenish the coffers of the Game Commission.

Apologists for the pod arrow call it a tranquilizer because the succinylcholine *is* used to tranquilize big game animals for live transport or study. However, it is normally used in liquid form in amounts of, for deer, 30 to 75 milligrams in solution of 20 milligrams to a cubic centimeter. The recommended dosage for the rubber sleeve known as the pod is from 300 to 700 milligrams in powder form. The tranquilizing dose will render the animal immobile even though it is fully conscious. The pod dose is designed to kill. It is reported that the body will absorb the heavier dose in about 15 minutes. If artificial respiration is applied during this period, assuming that someone is available and recognizes the problem, the afflicted organism will presumably recover.

To conclude this look at the pod arrow, my feelings are strongly

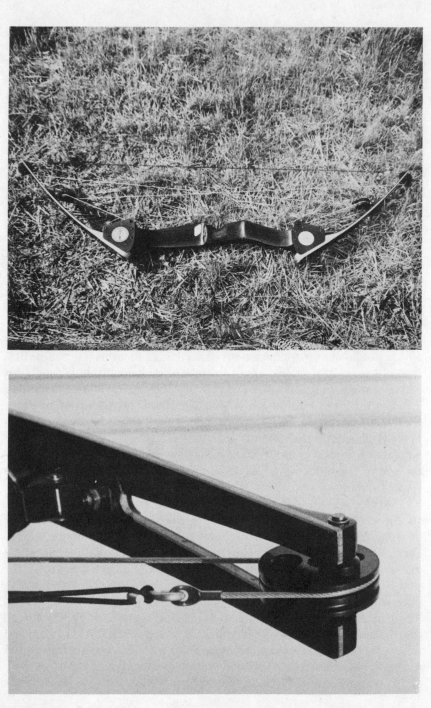

A Jennings compound bow with closeups of the unique attachments to this innovative arm.

A Jennings compound bow with closeups of the unique attachments to this innovative arm (continued).

opposed to it for the reasons cited. It has been suggested by some writers that other states should permit its use but not make it mandatory. I suggest that those who would first welcome its legalization are those who will not take the considerable time necessary to become proficient with the bow and arrow and hunt with it for the love of the sport.

A somewhat less controversial entry to the hunting scene in recent years is the compound bow. At this writing, five states and two provinces outlaw it, five states and three provinces have no regulations to cover it, one state has pending legislation to permit it, and all others have legalized its use.

The compound bow is the first real departure from basic bow dynamics since the first primitive weapon was invented possibly 50,000 years ago. Although the principle of the string and spring has been retained, the compound employs the use of pulleys and cables to store energy as two eccentric wheels at each end of the bow build, then relax draw pressure. For example, my compound bow draws 50 pounds going over the eccentrics and then relaxes to 38 pounds. Yet, upon release, full strength of the limbs, as they are set, is recovered.

Personal participation in chronograph tests proved the compound to be somewhat faster than comparable conventional recurved bows. An identical arrow was used in the tests. Since a lighter arrow can be used in the compound at the same weights as a conventional bow, it picks up a few more percentage points in speed.

On the plus side, the bow is extremely fast although somewhat less than most published reports in a direct comparison. Nevertheless, it does provide a flatter trajectory, a considerable advantage.

On the minus side, the bow is quite a bit heavier than most conventional bows. A broken string is a major repair job in the field, and it takes a certain amount of education to replace one. Aesthetically it turns some archers off since it is a departure from the beautiful form of a strung recurve bow.

It is an extremely good bow.

Most of the objections officially have come from those who fear that it is an encroachment upon the traditional concept of the bow. Although not so objectionable in itself, some fear that it will provide an opening for more advanced machinery until the romance associated with bow hunting will be subordinated to the search for better ways to kill. Whatever current reasons for objection, the compound as such appears to have become a permanent part of the hunting scene.

My sole objection is that some archers will be tempted to shoot at

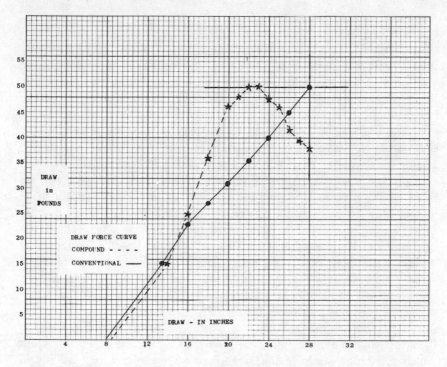

Draw force curve shows comparison between conventional and compound bow.

distances well beyond their personal abilities, but I am not critical of the inherent capabilities of the bow itself. Originated by H. W. Allen, of Kansas City, Missouri, who manufactures a hunting model under his name, the patents have been licensed to five other archery companies in the United States.

Fletching, the guidance system of an arrow, has traditionally been provided in this country by turkey feathers, easiest to obtain and fully practical. However, feathers are being challenged today by soft plastic vanes which are more weather resistant and somewhat quieter. Early stiff plastics, which became popular for slender target shafts, were not practical for heavier hunting arrows. Considerably longer and higher fletching is needed to guide the hunting shaft and to provide rotation to dampen any planing tendency caused by the heavy and comparably larger hunting head. Early plastic fletching would break passing the bow. This is not true of the newer soft plastics.

If you are guided by tradition and wish to use feather fletching, occasional application of one of the new moisture resistant agents will help weatherproof your feathers.

Gun hunters have been steered more and more toward bright clothing for their own protection. Some states now make it mandatory; more will follow. Since all big-game animals on this continent are color blind, it is a good safety measure. Why shouldn't the same rules be applied to bow hunting?

There are a number of sound reasons. It must be acknowledged that, although bright colors would reduce even the almost infinitesimal fatality rate among bow hunters, they just aren't practical. For, although such colors are seen as shades of gray to an animal, they are more readily *noticed*. Shooting the bow entails movement. Although an animal may not be unduly alerted by the object which a solid color presents, any movement would change the picture at once. This is no real problem for the gunner who can reach out literally hundreds of yards to his quarry. But, it is a severe handicap to a bow hunter trying to sneak off a shot at twenty or thirty yards—or less. Yet, I have killed a number of big-game animals as close as twelve yards while I was wearing a bright red and black *camouflage* suit.

The more camouflage you can effect, the better. It is important to break up your outline as much as possible. A jumbled pattern of color which resembles in shade the surrounding terrain and vegetation will greatly increase chances to stand and move undetected.

Think how many times, if you have hunted often, an animal has studiously looked you over if you were dressed in the usual gun-hunting attire. As soon as it figures you out, it either takes off or bunches its muscles for instant flight. Move, and you erase any doubts it might have. With a gun, you may still have an opportunity to drop it in its flight or get a standing shot if it stops to make another visual check.

Sometimes an archer will wear the latest in camouflage, smear his face with charcoal or camouflage paint, and then display a brightly colored club patch on his upper arm or wave a well-varnished bow that reflects every sunbeam.

There are several ways to camouflage a bow. I paint mine with auto primer and slash it with streaks of some other color such as yellow or brown. If you don't want to mess up the beautiful finish on your expensive bow, you can tape it, in strung position, with regular camouflage stick-on strips, or use masking tape, and then paint it. The only catch to this one is that, if the fiberglas starts to pull loose because of the tape, it will void the guarantee that comes with some bows.

Bow socks, camouflage-colored slipovers for each limb of the bow,

The more camouflage you can effect, the better.

will do the trick. But, they will impede the action of the bow to some degree, more if they become wet, and I just don't like them. But, they are available.

At this point, there is the hope that we are mentally, emotionally, and practically equipped to go for big game with the bow and arrow. Although there may be some points on which we are not in complete agreement, an attempt has been made to support recommendations and opinions offered. The only hope is that the reader will keep an open mind. Let's get on with it.

CHAPTER 3

Accessories

It is true that the basic essentials of a bow and arrow are all that are required for a successful hunt under certain circumstances. Many hunters in the better deer states have excellent opportunities within a very few miles of home. They know the terrain and vegetation so well that they can possibly do well without any extras other than what was presented in Chapter 2.

However, for the serious big-game bow hunter, who may have a pile of savings invested in an opportunity for one of the more hard-to-get trophies, anything that he can add to give him advantage is worth the investment. It is also worth the time to understand its use and to put it to best advantage.

Some of what follows may be considered optional extras to certain readers. But, the bow hunter who has spent a number of years at the sport might even come up with some additional extras which he considers essential to a good hunt.

Because some terms may not be familiar to all readers, a glossary of archery expressions is included in the back of this book. If you have any doubt about the meaning here, glance at the glossary. Since this is written chiefly for those who already have at least a speaking acquaintance with archery, the chapters will not be littered with definitions slowing down our approach to taking a big-game species with the bow and arrow.

One thing is important to consider when adding accessories to the bow limbs or the string. Each of them will slow down your arrow. This may vary from a few feet per second to a serious drop in power. It depends upon the type and the number. This may not seem important unless you add them up. Consequently, whatever accessories are to be used which can in any way affect the performance of your bow should be in place when you practice. Although the difference may not even be readily noticeable, a drop of even five feet per second on a bow which delivers a hunting arrow at 150 feet per second is a three and one-third percent efficiency loss. This can be the difference between a clean kill, a poor hit, or a miss, depending upon the distance involved.

If you are going to be hunting in brush or high grass, brush buttons or similar devices to keep twigs and other vegetation from getting caught between your bow string and the end of the limb are invaluable. String silencers, which can be anything from tied-on rubber bands to sophisticated plastic attachments, will help to quiet arrow release. This may allow a chance for a second shot, at best, or avoid having the animal jump the string at the release.

Whether to use a bow sight or not in big-game hunting is purely a matter of choice. However, behind the choice should be some studied thinking. Sights can be a handicap even to those who customarily utilize them in target practice. Use of conventional target sights require that the archer be able to know the distance so that his sight may be set for the shot. There is no one, to my knowledge, who can consistently judge distances well under field conditions and in the woods. Even with good shooting, improper selection of the sight marking can result in an off shot.

You can prove to yourself how difficult it is to judge distances. This is particularly so when only a single animal appears. A male animal, identified by its head adornment, immediately places itself in a general size category. For example, there isn't enough difference between a small buck deer and a large male animal to require much variance in the shot. However, with any deer species the archer must be aware of the approximate height of the males at the shoulders when making his educated guess as to yardage to his target.

If it is a female animal, the problem is magnified when the animal stands alone. Many a hunter, both with the gun and with the bow, has shot a deer of a size which normally wouldn't draw a second glance,

Sights can be effective if the bow hunter learns their use and sticks with them.

simply because it initially appeared so huge. If two small deer of equal size appear, it is also extremely difficult to determine their size unless there is some identifying feature such as visible buttons where antlers should be. Of course, if a doe and a fawn appear together, it is quite easy to note the difference in size.

The positive killing area on the average deer is approximately nine inches in diameter. The gold on the official 900 round which is shot at 40, 50, and 60 yards, is 9.6 inches in diameter. Those familiar with this target can quickly envision the difficulty of hitting the gold at distances beyond perhaps 30 yards with *hunting* tackle. If you are not acquainted with target shooting, consider the size of the average dinner plate as the kill area on a deer. It is true, of course, that killing shots are possible outside of this area, but let's think here in terms of the positive rather than the possible.

Since target bows are largely impractical for hunting, this would mean transferring the target sight to a hunting bow and setting up the equipment to give best results. But anyone willing to go to this much bother should take a look at some of the new hunting sights on the market.

There are sights which can be set by finger movement which will actually provide a system of range finding. They take a lot of practice to use and proper setting up, but they can be extremely deadly in the hands of a knowledgeable hunter.

The bowman who will take the time to install and calibrate the more common pin hunting sight properly through consistent practice has a distinct edge over a hunter without a sight. This is even more likely if he is using one with a built-in range finder. On the other hand, I have talked to a number of hunters who had sights on their bow and could not remember whether they used them on a successful shot.

The time it takes to guess at the distance and set a sight may give the quarry an opportunity to escape. Movement necessary for such

Some pre-calibrated sights can be adjusted to the proper distance by fingertip control.

adjustments may attract the animal's attention and again foul up the shot. Failure to use the sight properly can be much worse than using no sight at all. If you are going to be a sight shooter, stick with it. But, don't try to go back and forth between a bare bow and the sighted-in bow or you are asking for trouble and frustration.

Choice of a quiver, the receptacle to hold spare arrows, is important. It varies somewhat with the type of hunting planned and the species of animal sought.

If hunting is to be done from a solitary stand, it makes little difference what type of quiver is employed. If hunting entails considerable hiking, particularly if it is through thick bush, an entirely different quiver might be called for. Personally, my choice is for the quiver which attaches directly to the bow and one which will hold about eight arrows. It is the most convenient and fastest to use.

Above all, any quiver should be one which offers protection over the presumably sharp broadheads. In fact, I would like to see outlawed any quiver which does not have such a provision. Not only is the transport of unprotected arrowheads dangerous to the individual hunter, he risks stabbing his friends, cutting bow strings, ripping car upholstery, and anything else that is cutable or penetrable. There is no excuse for carrying arrows with their heads exposed with the fine quivers available today.

There are bow quivers designed so that they can screw onto the handle, or riser section, of a bow. Others are clip-on types. One thing to guard against with those which clip fast to the bow is to make sure that the ends of the attachment do not extend into the working part of the bow limb. Otherwise, it can have an effect upon the individual bow's shooting quality.

Most important considerations relative to bow quivers are whether or not they will transport easily through brush and whether they will hold sufficient arrows for a reasonable hunt. In areas where certain small game are in season concurrent with the big-game season, the archer may want to carry a couple target heads or blunts to shoot at such targets if they become available.

Although ideal for target shooting, the side quiver, which attaches to the belt at the hip, is completely impractical for most hunting. It is noisy, troublesome to get through brush, and it frequently gets out of position or falls off unless securely fastened down by a belt.

When on an extended hunting trip of a few days to a week or more, it is well to carry two knives. One can be an ordinary pocketknife for normal chores about camp. Some are satisfied to use such a knife

There are quivers adapted to all types of bow hunting as in this Colorado scene.

for skinning and dressing purposes. However, a good sheath knife, kept as sharp as possible, can be extremely handy when it comes to eviscerating or field dressing an animal. Without a separate pocketknife or small auxiliary sheath knife, there is too much temptation to use a regular hunting knife for chores which will dull its edge. In any event, any knife carried should be kept sharp for whatever purpose intended.

A length of nylon rope doesn't take up much space and can be invaluable. Its primary use would normally be to drag out a deer or other game which lends itself to this type of transport. Those who plan to pack in with their own horses or by foot need no education along this line. Others are more apt to be on guided hunts where the outfitter will provide the necessary rope.

But, the individual going back in some distance from camp or parking areas will still find that a strong rope can be of great help. It can either be used to drag the animal out or in fastening it to a carrying pole or for strapping animals to a back pack. Nylon dragging ropes can be purchased which have a loop at one end and a metal snap on the opposite end, which are quite handy.

Unless a hunter is in completely familiar territory, a compass should be standard equipment. It is useless, however, unless the owner

Handy items on a bow hunt: tissue paper, electrician's tape, dental tape, compass, pocketknife, sharpening stone, flashlight, drag rope, gloves, belt knife, plastic bag—all easy to carry.

knows how to utilize it. If you aren't familiar with the use of a compass, look up information on it or talk to someone who knows his way around.

In lieu of this, simply take a bearing when you leave familiar surroundings such as the camp or your automobile. Find out which way you are heading and know the opposite direction to get back. If you get confused, take the opposite reading of the direction in which you started out and keep walking. It is well then also to line up objects such as dead trees, rocks, stones, etc. which are in the same direction you want to follow. Each time you come to one of these selected landmarks, take a new reading and proceed along in that manner. You will at least end up somewhere in the vicinity of your starting point where there is certain to be a road or a stream that you can follow to help.

If you are in the deep bush or one of the remote parts of the United States, you are most likely to be with a qualified guide. In such instances, you will probably be given instructions as to what to do.

When confused about location, as an alternative sit tight, take care of yourself and try to get a smudge fire going so that you can be found. Absolutely the worst thing you can do is to panic and start heading off blindly in some random direction. You risk a fall, or becoming so lost that nobody can find you.

If possible, obtain a detailed map of the area you plan to hunt. These are available for most of the United States and Canada. Write to: Distribution Section, Geological Survey, 1200 South Eads St., Arlington, Virginia 22202, or to same at Federal Center, Denver, Colorado 80225.

No one should ever head into strange territory without a waterproof matchbox and/or a good cigarette lighter. Whether you smoke or not, a cigarette lighter is good insurance if you remember to keep it filled with fluid. As extras, several flints should be secreted under the first flap of cotton inside the lighter. In addition to this, you might obtain some of the substance now available which lights readily and will provide the nucleus of a warming fire or a smudge fire. A piece of stout candle is also good both for illumination and for starting fires if you become separated from your companions.

If possible, obtain a detailed map of the area that you plan to hunt.

Don't go hunting without a camera; taking two is better.

Don't go hunting without a camera. There is always some scene or some incident that you will want to record for the later pleasure of reviewing it. If you are thinking in terms of telephoto lenses, wide angle lenses, etc., you don't need any further help here. But, if you are not well acquainted with cameras, buy a good 35mm camera of simple operation so that you don't deny yourself this extra satisfaction of having a pictorial record of your trip.

Hunting heads must be sharp. Depending upon how they are transported to your hunting ground and the type of quiver you use, there is always a certain hazard to the razor edge that you have filed or honed onto your broadheads. This, plus the fact that you may be tempted to take some practice shots in addition to those at game can be rough on your hunting heads. A small file is a right handy item to have in camp.

A small pack of toilet or cleansing tissue is practically a must. There are all sorts of uses to which such can be put including those for which they were designed. In addition to the more obvious uses, such paper can serve to wipe one's hands after field dressing an animal. It can be used to mark trail when tracking a wounded animal. It can be used to mark your own trail if you become lost so that you can return to the starting point or provide a guide for those looking for you. It can be used to dry off tackle after a rain or a snow storm.

A roll of one-inch sterile gauze is a fairly efficient first aid kit for normal wear and tear on the anatomy. Folded pieces of it can be used as a compress while the rest is wrapped around to hold it in place. It can be used to bind up a cut until professional attention is available. A few adhesive bandages are handy for lesser mishaps while on the trail. A fairly complete first aid kit should be kept at camp or in the automobile, particularly when in the more remote territories. A neckerchief or large bandanna handkerchief has many uses and can be used as a sling or a tourniquet in the event of a mishap. These can now be purchased in camouflage colors.

Don't carry a white handkerchief. In the gunning season, a white object is too easily mistaken for a deer's rump or tail, particularly in whitetailed deer country.

Since special bow hunting seasons usually come before the gunning season in most areas, the weather will probably be warm. There is a limit to the extras you can comfortably carry. Go light. But, depending upon the territory and how far you plan to travel from your base, don't skip anything which might be essential to your safety or a proper follow-through on a successful hunt.

If you are optimistic, a fairly stout plastic bag can be extremely useful to save and carry the heart and liver of your quarry. Knowledgeable hunters recognize these as some of the tastiest parts of most big game animals.

If you still have some room remaining, a welcome addition is some well-packaged, melt-proof chocolate. It provides quick energy if you don't make it back for a meal. Or, it may have more meaningful use if you don't make it at all until you are found or can work your way back the next morning.

A good binocular can be a considerable asset. But, it must be one small enough to fit into a pocket or which can be carried under your presumably camouflaged outer clothing. If carried inside the clothing, it must be in a position where it will not interfere with a shot; it must clear the bow string.

Although useful primarily in the western United States where glassing the wide open spaces will frequently reveal game, I carry one wherever I hunt. Even in the brush areas of the Northeast it has its uses. Most important, of course, is to spot game. But, it can also be handy to identify hunters at a distance if you are in a party. It can help pass the time on a stand if used with care so that movement doesn't defeat the purpose of the hunt. Bringing a squirrel or a chipmunk or a woodchuck up close to observe is a special plus value when out-of-doors.

A proper binocular is not cheap. But, there are a number of excellent ones on the market today that fit the bow hunter's pocket and pocketbook.

In the preceding, accessories range from necessities down to pleasurable extras. What you take you must carry. Where you hunt will have some bearing on what is considered necessary. Experience will dictate your list after a few hunts.

CHAPTER 4

Planning a Hunt

Planning a hunt can be anything from, "What time do you want me to pick you up, Joe?", to making application for a drawing many months before the season opens.

Prior to writing this chapter my last deer hunt was about an airline mile from home. During the late archery season in January there had been a herd of six whitetails in the area. Five of them showed, out of range, to provide a fitting finale to a season in which my score was zero on the home range. It was spoiled when I found the sixth deer, a yearling buck, lying dead with a bullet through its chest not more than 150 yards from my last stand.

Obviously, it didn't take much preparation for that hunt. Just slip into a camouflage suit, grab the quiver-equipped bow, and take the car. From plan to stand took a total of about ten minutes.

However, a hunt the previous September some 1600 miles to Wyoming took literally months of planning and preparation. My oldest son, Keith, and I both applied for licenses to hunt mule deer and antelope early in the spring. Then we had to sweat out the drawing to determine if both of us would receive tags to hunt these animals and in the area we wanted, Jim Zerbst's Boggy Creek Ranch in the east central part of the state. Meanwhile, there were such things as arranging air reservations, auto pickup at the Rapid City, South Dakota airport; choice of clothing and footwear; maps; etc.

Everything came off—almost as planned. We arrived a day too early when our contact read the calendar wrong. It worked out okay, however, since it gave us a day to study the area and to take pictures. It also gave us time to drive to Lusk to pick up a $5.00 archery tag for each hunting permit. We weren't even aware that we needed them!

This and many bow hunting trips to other states and Canadian provinces, aside from prompting this book, made an appendix to it a must. Although proper planning to hunt in other than your resident state should always include contact with game officials, the appendix will give you an insight regarding what to expect. It is the result of a survey covering all of the states and the eleven Canadian provinces. Except for Northwest Territories where no bow hunting of any kind was permitted as of February, 1973, all recognize the bow and arrow as a proper hunting combination. Nevertheless, no two political subdivisions have identical laws.

Three states, Illinois, Iowa and Kansas, permit resident bow hunting but make no provision for nonresidents. Some provide a special archery tag at a cost lower than for the gun-hunting license. Others require that you buy a full hunting license which makes it permissible to hunt with either bow or gun. Cost to hunt runs from a low of $10.25 in Rhode Island to a high of $151.00 in Montana. You may find that you pay a sizable sum for a license and then must pay extra to hunt for a particular game species and are charged a trophy fee on top of that if you make a kill. In some areas, you are only permitted to shoot the particular animal for which you are licensed. Others, such as Pennsylvania where the visitor tag is $42.55 of which $2.00 is for the archery permit, gives you the privilege of hunting for anything in season.

That's only part of it.

There are 37 states and four provinces which dictate the minimum size broadhead that may be used. Most that have regulations require no less than the $7/8''$ width. But, some want a minimum of $3/4''$. Six states even set the minimum length of the broadhead at $1\frac{1}{2}''$. Reference has been made previously to the fact that some states still outlaw the compound bow. Only a handful have no rules against the poison arrow with but one, Alaska, actually legalizing it. And, two states, Alaska and Wyoming, and four provinces, permit the crossbow.

Minimum bow weights run from 30 pounds to 45 pounds for deer.

Two states and four provinces permit the crossbow for hunting.

Oregon and Wyoming require no less than 50 pounds for the larger game species. Several states and one province set the arrow length at 24″; Oklahoma requires 28″; Oregon, 437½ grains minimum weight.

Most of these rulings make little or no sense to an experienced bow hunter. It is the belief here that they became law in the early days of modern bow hunting before the advent of more sophisticated tackle and knowledge about the bow and arrow. It is hoped that as states and provinces revise their laws or write new ones, a more studied approach will be given to the need or lack of need for such details.

Certainly there is no intent here to suggest how individual state or province seasons should be set or what prices should be placed on hunting licenses. However, there appears to have been a race in recent years to either discourage nonresident hunting or to price the common man out of the picture. For, this is the effect of high price tags on nonresident permits. If the desire is to keep wild game for resident sportsmen, possibly it would be better simply to eliminate nonresident licenses. But, when states that depend largely upon nonresidents to support their fish and game programs continue to increase the cost, the higher prices for licenses is self-defeating. The license cost is only a small part of the total money spent by visiting sportsmen.

Among the assorted regulations governing tackle, the only one which makes much sense is that of minimum bow weight. But, then only if the archer is capable of drawing it with *his* hunting arrow. It has always been my personal feeling that 40 pounds should be the minimum weight at full draw for animals up to the size of a deer. And, no less than 50 pounds should be permitted for larger game species.

The reasoning behind this eliminates those instances in which such animals have been taken with target-weight bows.

In the excitement of the moment, in crowding brush or with uncertain footing, a bowman may not come to full draw. The preceding minimums will probably still give him enough thrust needed to put his arrow into the quarry. If the distance is close enough, the spare power may still permit a clean kill. Add to these frequent handicaps the tendency to creep, to permit a muscle letdown at the instant before release so that part of the power is lost, and the need for more than barely minimum power becomes evident.

As to broadheads, the obvious need has resulted in products on the market today that meet most minimums. Trying to pin the minimum width to exactly ⅞″ or ¾″ doesn't fit the picture. To repeat a previous thought, surely it is better to have a *sharp* head a fraction under the minimums than one twice as wide that is dull. Repeated sharpening of a legal head of marginal width could make it illegal.

Length of a broadhead has little relevance since a well-balanced head normally exceeds the 1½″ required by some states. Anyway, how is the head to be measured? Is it the cutting edge? Is it the distance from point to base of blade? Base of sleeve? Where? The rules aren't specific.

Again, a minimum arrow length, per se, has no relevance whatsoever. If an archer can get 50 pounds out of a 25″ arrow, he is well set up for big game. On the other hand, he would be hunting illegally in Oklahoma where the minimum bow weight is 40 pounds, but a 28″

arrow must be used. An archer who can't draw 28 inches is using an incorrect arrow at that length!

Regardless of any personal feelings on the subject or how you may feel about some of the regulations, they must be respected. This is another good reason to take the preceding into your planning. Officers must swear to uphold the law. There is little worse to turn the pleasure of a hunt into a better-to-be-forgotten trip than a brush with the law. It is our responsibility to know the law when we hunt as a paying guest in an area with unfamiliar rules.

Trying to pick an outfitter familiar with the special needs of bow hunters is sometimes difficult. Any game department can give you a list of outfitters, but it is wise to state that you plan to hunt with the bow. Since officialdom is reluctant to make specific recommendations, you may have to settle for a general list. Read such lists carefully. If the outfitter specializes in bow hunting, he will usually so state.

If it becomes necessary to take whatever outfitter is available, make certain that he understands your special requirements. In most areas where guides are required, you will be hunting against the guns. If the outfitter has had previous experience with archers, he can anticipate your needs. If he doesn't guide you himself, he will likely hire guides who can do a proper job.

It is the bow hunter's responsibility to know the law when hunting in an unfamiliar area.

The need for either or both, an understanding outfitter and a guide, cannot be overemphasized. Those who regard bow hunting with a somewhat jaundiced eye should be avoided. Or, the fellow who can practically guarantee you success should be suspect. You know the problems in bow hunting. All you can and should expect is that you will be placed in a position where you have a reasonable chance to score.

This sounds like a simple order. But right here is where most archery-inexperienced guides fall short. They are so used to having the average gun hunter shoot at any reasonable distance up to 500 yards that they are pleased with themselves if they can get you to within 100 yards of your quarry. Normally, that is where the hunt with the bow is just starting.

In the north country, where the bow is still frequently a novelty, guides have urged me to, "Shoot, shoot," at distances of 100 yards and beyond. The same holds true at times when the range is reasonable, but I don't like the angle for the shot. Guides can get upset. They think in terms of a healthy tip if their hunter scores. Unfortunately, in the bush country, an animal represents food and little more to many guides who work with hunters and fishermen in season and may take a holiday or employment with a lumber company during the winter.

At times language is a problem no matter how good a guide is provided for you. Indians and Canadian Frenchmen are not always conversant in English. In such instances, be sure through an interpreter that the guide understands your needs exactly.

Whether you are employing an outfitter or not, be sure that you know what weather might reasonably be expected where you plan your hunt. Even so, go equipped for 20 or 30 degrees either side of the usual temperature. You can always remove clothing if the weather is unseasonably warm, but you can't add clothing that you don't have.

Bulky clothing should be avoided unless you have practiced long and well wearing it. Since pre-season bow practice is usually done mostly in warm or cool weather, few are going to go through such torture. This does not eliminate the excellent insulated clothing today available. But you will do well to take several vests or light jackets so that you can avoid bulk and also be in a position to add or subtract according to the temperature.

Never overdress. It is better to be on the cool side before exercise than to load up so that you are as snug as when traveling to the outside john. Otherwise, you will heat up on the first steep grade and build a layer of perspiration. When it becomes necessary to stand or wait out an animal, that sweat can turn to ice water. Keep in mind that a camou-

Dress according to the temperatures expected where you plan to hunt.

flage suit serves somewhat as a windbreaker. If you are wearing thermal underwear, it won't take much between your camouflage and that underwear to keep fairly comfortable in all but the most inclement weather. Anyway, you don't want your bow arm bunched up with unneeded clothing that can catch your bow string.

Possibly I am a poor one to give advice on clothing. I always wear summer underwear, a camouflage suit, up to two pairs of summer trousers, up to two cotton and wool shirts, and a light insulated vest and/or a light insulated jacket. In October, north of the Mason and Dixon Line, up to the Canadian border, I frequently eliminate all but one pair of pants, the underwear and the camouflage suit. An Indian ancestor apparently passed down to me a good thermostat.

But, my heritage didn't include good recommendations for footwear. Moccasins may have been fine for my great, great grandmother, but there is much better footwear for hunting today. And, of all items of attire, footwear is the most important.

The worst mistake anyone can make is to buy and wear a new pair of boots or shoes for a hunt without first breaking them in properly. It is much better to take a pair of old leaky shoes that you know are comfortable than to risk breaking in a leakproof pair on a hunt.

Here again personal preference and need enters the picture. I pre-

Of all items of attire, comfortable, broken-in footwear is the most important. Keep it waterproofed.

fer insulated soft leather shoes that reach an inch or two above the ankle. There are some that won't leak for a year with proper care. This doesn't prevent water from coming in over the tops. However, you can walk the water out of shoes if they are comfortable—the best way to dry them. A spare pair is nevertheless a good idea on an extended hunt. And, my preference is for summer stockings or socks, two pairs if it gets cold. Some previous leg problems require that I wear knee-length hose so that there is not the common problem of having them slip down inside the shoes even if they become wet.

Some prefer rubber bottoms with leather tops. The only hooker to this is that rubber induces perspiration. Once your feet become wet, through perspiration or immersion, they stay that way.

Those who feel sorry for me when we start out before daybreak when dew is heavy in autumn frequently direct their pity to themselves before the day is over. Even wet trousers can leak water down inside low footwear.

The only alternatives are knee-length leather or rubber boots and waterproof pants. They are great for moose hunting in marshes, but they are a dead giveaway if you are trying to sneak up on a whitetailed deer in the heavy brushland of the Northeast.

I have hunted in sneakers when the weather permitted. Even

painted a pair black for the purpose. But, if much walking is involved, you run the risk of a sprained or a broken ankle with so little support. Too, since there is little heel support in such footwear, there is a real risk of pulling or straining tendons or ligaments, injuries which can be tougher to cure than a break.

Since wet feet are a part of hunting, extra hose are important. In fact, it is well to carry an extra pair in a pocket so that you can change if the weather continues wet and you can't depend upon body heat to dry out your foot gear.

Rain and wet snow can be a problem. A light drizzle may be fine for stalking since the air is usually still and your movements are muffled. But, some sort of rain gear is certainly handy if you plan to hunt far from your base. You won't do much hunting in it anyway, but it can get you back to your bunk fairly dry if you get caught in a drencher. My choice for such emergencies is a cheap, extremely lightweight slicker that will fit into a pocket with my extra hose.

It is rare that you can be really comfortable physically when hunting. Too often you are brushing sweat and/or bugs out of your eyes or shaking snow out of your collar or seeking a big tree for shelter so that you can don your rain gear.

Today, more and more hunters are traveling by air. The time saved in travel provides more time for hunting. And, today there are areas to hunt which require flying back into the bush to some lake or river even though you might reach your point of departure by car or train.

One of the bow hunter's problems arises from the air hijacking contingency. Airline personnel are not knowledgeable about the bow and arrow. Even though a bow without an arrow is no more dangerous than a stick of like dimensions, some will not permit a bow in other than the baggage compartment of a plane. Consequently, it is important that both your bow and your arrows be packaged to avoid damage. Airline baggage handlers are notorious for their disregard of other people's property. There is also the problem of transporting your tackle in bush planes which might vary in size from a large twin-engined transport down to a Piper Cub. Personally, I never go on an extended trip with less than two bows suitable for the hunting expected.

Takedown bows today have been perfected to a degree that they are as reliable as conventional tackle. Use of one is almost a must for any archer who hunts extensively out of his own area, from the standpoint of travel alone.

Since seasons dictate the times within a relatively short period that one can go hunting, airline reservations should be made early. Check

Bush planes may vary from a large twin-engined transport down to a Piper Cub. This is Squaw Lake, Upper Quebec.

schedules carefully. Recently I was able to save $60.00 on one flight by inquiring about other than the route proposed to me by the ticket agency. Check reservations a couple of days before departure. You will be paying for time on your hunt in most cases even if you arrive late.

That brings up another point. When you contract for a hunt of five or seven days, or whatever, you pay for the full hunt even though you score in the first five minutes. It is well to investigate the fishing or other species of game that can be hunted so that you don't have to sit around with time on your hands. For, even if you decide to leave after downing your trophy, you usually won't get a deduction on your bill.

Be certain that you have a perfect understanding with your outfitter. Know what he will furnish and what you are expected to bring in the way of bedding. If a sleeping bag is required, buy one to match the temperature. Also, know what you are paying for, particularly if flying is involved. Usually, the day of arrival and the day of departure are considered as one day.

Tipping is a touchy subject. Of course, you shouldn't tip your outfitter. A guide is something else. It is a good idea to ask your outfitter on the quiet what the guides usually get for a successful hunt or for just a good effort. He will likely quote you the high and the low. This is a matter of personal discretion. You don't *have* to tip anything, particularly if you get a poor hunt. The guide is being paid. Some, however, get spoiled by wealthy hunters and expect too much. Or, in the flush of downing a trophy, some hunters are so happy that they tip more than they can afford and make it rough on the next hunter. It is a typical American weakness. If you have different guides on different days, split the regular tip.

I have had guides ranging from illiterate backwoodsmen to college professors and students picking up some extra money. Most are hired because they are woods-wise; others are picked because no one else is available. Most will knock themselves out for you. Packing out a big-game animal in quarters is tough work anytime, anywhere. A wounded moose that takes to water to die provides a real chore. A goat or a sheep carcass high in the rocks of thin air and uncertain weather presents its own special problems. You may have thought that the guide had easy going until you look down on that elusive trophy that now represents anywhere from half a day to two days work just getting it back to camp.

Do a little bookwork before you leave home on the best cuts of meat. For, you may not be able to bring all of it back with you, particularly if you fly. Some guides will try to get away with just bringing out the four quarters. Tasty chops and loins become wolf bait. Do some advance planning as to how you can get as much meat home as possible. It will help pay for your trip. Even the cost of flying home the better cuts of meat is substantially less than its actual worth. Besides, there is something special in sitting down to a dinner provided through your own skill as a hunter. It completes the story of what hunting is all about even though it is a minor part of the whole.

Much of the preceding has centered around a commercial package in big-game hunting. In many cases, it is the only way to go because of travel and camp logistics. Unless you are a year-around outdoorsman with a full complement of camping cover and tools and the knowledge to go with them, it is the best way to go. If you are one of the rare types well equipped with experience and gear, you don't need any help. Unless, of course, you want to take a holiday from camp chores and go for a commercial package.

What has been presented here applies equally for the gun hunter with a few exceptions. For instance, weather is generally rougher in the gunning season where the bow and gun periods don't run consecutively. And, of course, some of the information is for bow hunters alone as with bow and arrow regulations.

However, when it comes to the actual planning and hunting, the gunner who follows procedures which work for archers may find that his score will improve substantially, and he will get much more enjoyment from his hunt.

In local or area hunts, conditions in the particular part of the country pretty much outline requirements for those involved. They are as many and as varied as the terrain and the weather. Since most archers have previously had at least an association with gunning, they know better what is required in their section than any one individual could suggest.

What has been written here about pre-planning is chiefly for those who hunt far afield. But, the basic requirements don't vary too much from place to place.

CHAPTER 5

Basic Hunting Methods

As a one-time and sometimes gun hunter, I often find a considerable overlap in my thinking about hunting with the bow. Like most bow hunters, my early experiences were primarily associated with the gun for both small and large game. For a time the bow was a secondary pleasure until favored choice of arms was reversed in my hunting.

Today, about the only times that a gun comes off my rack is when I get hungry for pheasants, fried rabbit, or stewed squirrel. My score on these with the bow seldom adds up to much for dinner. Or, if the muskrats start to tunnel through the dike on my fishing pond, I grab a rifle or a shotgun for this serious business. Maybe it is just a water snake that needs eliminating to save my bullfrogs. In such instances, I use a gun.

But frequently when carrying a bow the thought keeps coming up about what a comparatively lousy hunter I was before taking to the bow and arrow. Although my score was respectable on deer, the only large game taken with the gun, had I tried as hard and as carefully as when later carrying the bow, it would have been far better. Many times during the gunning season in more recent years, I have had opportunities that would have been fairly certain had I not been carrying a bow. Yet, even at quitting time on the last day of the seasons in which my score has been zero, there are no regrets. Bow hunting has so much more to offer than another notch on my record stick.

Nevertheless, the fact remains that gunners who follow the same methods necessary to a reasonable chance for success with the bow, are almost certain to improve their records. So, if you alternate arms in seasons for big game, you certainly can't hurt your score by adopting some of the methods forced upon archers who take their bow hunting seriously. It must be kept in mind that what works in bow hunting will work at least equally well in gun hunting, but the reverse is not necessarily true.

It is somewhat axiomatic that methods in hunting with the bow today are little or no different than those practiced by primitive man. From the crudest aborigine on each of the continents where the bow originated or was imported before recorded history, up through the American Indian, little has changed in basic hunting techniques.

This is interesting in this day of moon trips and hydrogen bombs; man again accepts most of the handicaps in his *hunting* with the bow that Nature imposed upon his unknown ancestors. The same handicaps are still imposed upon his brothers of the bush in more remote parts of the world. Of course, modern tackle, clothing, transportation, communications and biological familiarity are built-in advantages in our approach. But, the basic game of hide and seek has changed not one whit since the bow began. Herein lies the real fascination of bow hunting.

What the primitives lacked in the previously mentioned modern advantages, they made up in woods lore. After all, they hunted in completely familiar environments; their homes were constructed of natural materials, their highways were beaten paths through the fields and forests; their senses were tuned to their surroundings. Besides, they were hungry.

Our attempt is merely to even the odds as much as possible to satiate our appetite for sport. The archer who spends a small fortune for a hunt in the knowledge that he can't afford to have much, if any, of the meat hauled home, and must give it away to the Eskimos or the Indians, or whomever, serves a different hunger than that of his belly. Not only that, he might miss!

But, in the various approaches to bow hunting, there is food for the thrill-fashioned receptacles of man's mind to compensate for failure to claim his intended quarry. A black bear bumbling through a deer drive, a fawn stretching its inquisitiveness toward a motionless hunter, a low gaggle of geese noisily gathering customers for a trip south at the expense of your solitary stand, a red fox tripping daintily by on a serious errand of gustatory necessity, a dead leaf undulating its way noisily among the limbs toward its reunion with earth—how many ways do you count success? Yet, what brought you here is an instinct that once didn't allow for such pleasures. Only a kill could compensate for the time spent.

Nevertheless, there is nothing quite like winning. We can succeed without winning; but no matter how wonderful the scenery, we want to sometime reach our goal. Reminiscences are individually the sum of one memorable experience.

Basically, there are three methods of hunting. Whether you are throwing rocks or using an elephant gun, one of these methods must be employed to get you into position to utilize the projectile upon which depends the outcome of your endeavor. They are: still hunting, driving, and stalking.

Which method is employed in bow hunting is dependent somewhat upon the number of hunters involved, terrain, and the quarry itself. In one day's hunt, all three methods might come into play. A group of deer hunters might start out by each taking a stand to still hunt before daylight, get together at an appointed hour to drive, and one or more might end up stalking a particular animal during the drive before the group disbands in late afternoon to again take individual stands.

However, since still hunting is the most widely used method, we will take a look at it first.

Still hunting was undoubtedly the first method of hunting employed by the earliest primitives. There is evidence that man first confined his association to family groups through distrust of his neighbors and the instinct for survival before developing a gregarious nature. He had no choice but to hunt alone. Predators that hunt alone must make some provision to utilize the kill. In other than the maternity period, some animal predators will cover their kill to return and feed when necessary. When there is more than one mouth to feed, there must be some provision to bring home the bacon.

Since man biologically hasn't changed much, he had to make his big game kills somewhere in the vicinity of his domestic abode, transportation being what it was. This was necessary especially when his spouse wasn't in traveling condition. What better circumstance then in which to learn the trails and the habits of his quarry?

The domestic scene has altered somewhat, but the methods of lying in wait haven't changed.

Still hunting is the most common method used by bow hunters.

Probably the primary clue in still hunting is to know the traveling habits of the quarry being sought. Such habits are somewhat governed by climatic conditions at the time. If the season is dry, animals must drink. Except in areas of no surface water where they must depend upon dew and rain puddles, such as on the island of Hawaii, daily game movements will be determined by available water. When spring runs and potholes dry up, main watering holes will be visited daily.

Animals such as deer will move to areas of good feed for night foraging. This is particularly true in farming country. However, even in the mountains, all big-game species will usually seek out both feed and water toward night since they frequently go together. And, they must return.

If it is the breeding season, a mating call can bring the quarry by or to your stand. This will depend upon whether you are doing the calling or attempting to intercept the game when it responds to calls made by someone else or by its natural mate.

Depending upon the time of year, certain animals will move from one locality to another to avoid approaching winter. Frequently they travel well-worn trails, a natural spot for a still hunter to intercept them.

But, no matter what reasoning is behind choice of stands for a still hunt, such things as air movement, cover and quiet enter into each selection. There is a reason for placing them in this sequence, for it is in the same order of importance to most animals.

Even though you know the movement pattern of the game being sought, it is equally important to guess the movement of air correctly at your chosen stand. In the northern hemisphere, prevailing winds are from the west. But, in the approach of a low pressure system which frequently brings a change in weather, air movements will continue to change as the system moves in. Air travels counterclockwise around a low. However, this is governed by the direction from which the low pressure system is approaching. Hence it may move through 360° of the compass over a period of time. If there are signs of a change, it is well to have several spots picked out in advance in the event it is necessary to move from one to another to be sure your scent will be carried away from approaching game.

Contrariwise, if the weather has been on the sour side, a high pressure system, which usually brings clear skies, will have opposite air movements. That is, air moves clockwise around a high pressure system.

At times there is little you can do about it, particularly if the terrain is such that you have only one vantage point. In such cases, try to keep above the trail being watched. The air may carry your scent over the animal or at least break it up so that your position can't be pinpointed by a sensitive nose.

If the air is still, or nearly so in early morning or late afternoon, there are nevertheless imperceptible shifts of air in mountainous country. As the sun starts to warm the air, it rises. This is to the hunter's advantage since animals normally are moving from low pastures and water to bedding spots on the higher benches.

In the afternoon, as the air cools, it descends the slopes. Again, the hunter gets an advantage if he plans in advance.

Although all animals have their senses developed to a degree which best fits their life pattern, the sense of smell is most highly developed in all mammals. It must be taken into consideration when hunting any species of big game. Sight is most finely tuned in those creatures which are natural prey to others. And, while hearing is extremely sensitive in all of the creatures we hunt, it is the least dependable of the senses prompting the animal's decision toward escape or efforts toward aggression. Were this not true, it would be impossible to lure certain of the quarry through calls which simulate their kind or their natural prey.

Keen vision possessed by most animals presents the hunter with a problem at all times. To the gun hunter with long-range capabilities, it is much less a problem than with the archer who must get close to his quarry. But, it should be considered that hunter movement is the surest giveaway, much more detrimental to success than lack of cover or personal camouflage. Before the awareness of camouflage was prompted by World War II, we hunted in whatever clothing we had appropriate to weather conditions and the temperature. We still managed to get fairly close to game, but it required the utmost stealth.

I recall wearing a favorite yellow sweat shirt in temperate weather. Deer would approach quite close. But, the moment I moved the slightest, the animal would be gone. As long as I remained motionless, the deer would not become alarmed unless it just happened to look my way. For a moment, it would be attracted just to the break in the pattern of the background, but then it would identify *my* pattern and spook with a scramble though I didn't even breathe.

Use of camouflage clothing changed all this. The deer will look me over now and then continue about their business as long as I don't *move*. It doesn't matter whether I am wearing green or red camouflage. Personal experience supports the belief that animals of North America are color-blind. And, I simply will not hunt against the guns wearing other than red camouflage.

Although animals depend considerably upon their excellent hearing, there is much evidence that it is the least reliable of their senses when pitted against man's cunning. They hear you. But their interpretation of what they hear is frequently faulty. It is only when a hunter makes a sound which is unfamiliar to the creature that it becomes really alert. A cigarette lighter jangling against a pocketknife or loose change, an accidentally dropped arrow with the metal head clattering on a rock, a sneeze or cough, the human voice—these are sounds that will spook an animal much more quickly than breaking a twig, dislodging a stone or dropping something on the leaves. The human voice carries amazing distances. Even though it may not spook an animal, it will alert it to your presence.

None of the sounds will escape the animal's attention. But, only those which do not occur naturally will attract more than its passing interest. If you remain motionless, most times you can get away with noises which could just as easily have been caused by another animal or a bird.

But, if even a trace of scent is carrying toward your quarry, and you move or make a sound which attracts its attention to you and you are not well camouflaged, forget it! Or, plan on a long wait until another animal strays your way.

One of the best moose callers I know sounds like a sick calf, but he gets results. This only emphasizes that anyone who can learn to use a turkey or an animal call has a chance of success even if his calling is imperfect, whatever that is. Who knows what a perfect call really is? Of course, the closer you can simulate the sounds that emanate from the creature being hunted, the better chance you have of succeeding. It is not difficult to get a response to a call; getting the target to move within shooting range is another matter.

I don't know what turkeys think of my calling, but they respond. One day I was calling for a gun hunter and had a gobbler moving. When I thought it was about time for a shot, my hunter appeared. He finally confessed that he thought it was another hunter answering my call and he exposed himself to a fine bird. Apparently he figured that both the turkey and I were liars.

It is reported that rattling up bucks by banging a pair of old antlers together is successful in the Southwest. I don't know of anyone who is successful at it in the East. Blowing on a reed or a piece of rubber band is supposed to bring in deer. When hunting with the bow, the less attention I attract to myself the better I like it. This is not to discount any such methods, but I have no personal experience to support them.

The same for scents. For years there were advertisements of lures which would bring animals running in to be shot. I tried one. In fact, I forgot to take the bottle home with me and went back to pick it up several days later. Despite the fact that the lure sat on a log with the cap off along a much-used deer trail, it was still sitting where I had left it. It would seem that some deer would have at least muzzled the bottle off its precarious position had it been a good attractant.

Possibly there is a clue in the fact that today most advertisements merely claim that scents cover up human odors. This seems more likely. But, again, if you have something going for you, stick with it.

Whether you are taking a solitary stand or are awaiting drivers ostensibly bringing game to you, the question arises as to whether a tree stand or a ground stand is the better.

Some excellent elevators have been invented with which you can climb a tree; screw-in steps are available, or you can build a stand. You can also climb a tree on your own, of course. Damaging trees for hunting is frowned upon by government officials and many private owners. So, unless you have permission to do some chopping or nailing,

Some excellent tree stands have been devised which will not injure the tree as this one used by Sherwood Schoch.

all that is left are the seats which can be worked up a tree, or your own climbing ability.

Alternatives are natural or artificial blinds, or the ability to stand or sit quietly in one spot. Building blinds of natural cover again may put you in conflict with public or private owners. To avoid this, carry your blind with you. Or, carry some camouflaged netting with you to drape over low limbs or bushes for concealment. If none of these appeal to you, try for a spot which will best hide your form and still leave you the freedom of movement to take a shot if one becomes available. Avoid backdrops of contrasting color which will be more apt to reveal any movement you make even though the actual color is not distinguishable by your quarry. Above all, don't stand on the skyline.

One of the most important things to remember when standing along an animal runway or trail is the probable angle of your shot. Head-on shots are difficult; you are more apt to be seen. So, as long as you can visually cover the trail, don't worry about your shot until the animal is broadside or slightly angled away from you. The angle shot is better since the animal's best vision will have passed your station. It is less apt to notice your movement at draw of the bow. Or, you may be able to get to full draw unseen during the animal's approach. But don't wait too long or you will have a difficult shot to make. Be ready to release at a few paces past the broadside position.

Even though the animal may not spook if it sees the slight movement as you draw, it will have detected your presence. It may jump the string at the shot, the result being a poor hit or a complete miss. This is particularly true of such spring-loaded creatures as deer and antelope.

Whether your stand is for a morning or an evening hunt is a factor of almost as much importance as air movement. In mountainous areas or when staking out a water hole, whether the animal is approaching an area of relative danger or returning to an area of relative safety makes a great difference. It is likely to be extremely cautious when leaving the safety of tall grass or timber to expose itself while grazing or drinking. It will spook at the least hint of danger. On the other hand, when it is returning to these havens it is more likely to move boldly or merely stop inquiringly if something seems suspicious.

When it comes to a choice between tree stands and terra firma, my personal selection is for the dirt, every time.

Foremost among the reasons for this personal preference is simply the angle of the shot. It is easier to reach the vitals of an animal from its own level than from a higher position. Body cavity blood will much more quickly reach the area of arrow penetration and provide a trail than from a hit down into the body cavity from above. A ground level shot also offers a larger target of the vital areas. If the downward hit does not effect complete penetration, there may be very little blood trail until the animal has traveled for some distance—possibly too far for its recovery, particularly in the heavy foliage of early autumn or late summer.

My second reason for choice of a ground stand is because of greater mobility. You have a relatively small area that can be covered from a high seat or stand. If the game decides to take a different trail or feed under a different apple tree than the one you are watching, you have had it for that period. When on the ground, you do have a chance to change positions if the situation warrants it. Conversely, perhaps only a slight change in air movement may negate your chance to score from the choicest tree stand.

A minor reason, but one which has more serious personal implications, is simply that I get sleepy if I remain too long in one position. I recall asking for rope on one Maine bear hunting foray when I was actually fearful of dozing and falling from a high platform.

But, if you like to be elevated, use care in getting to and from your high chair. Be sure to carry a rope or stout string so that you can pull your bow and arrows up *after* you are safely in your tree stand. Further, use the same help to lower your tackle *before* you descend. No one should consider a tree stand without plenty of prior practice from that position.

The only Pennsylvania bow hunting fatality on record at this writing occurred when an archer dropped his arrows to the ground. One landed nock first and stuck upright. When the hunter jumped or fell from the tree, that arrow pierced his thigh. He bled to death while in his car driving for help.

Always keep an arrow on the string when game is expected. For this reason alone it is well to have nocks which, when the bow is held horizontally, will barely support an arrow on the string without the help of a hand or finger. There are commercial gadgets available, known as arrow holders, that will hold an arrow in shooting position without other assistance until it is drawn an inch or so, whereupon the gadget disengages. If a convenient bow quiver is not being used, extra arrows should be readily available in the event of a chance for a second shot.

There are those who discourage smoking when on a stand. Usually, the reason given is that the quarry will smell the smoke. If it can smell the smoke, which may or may not cause it to spook, it can probably also smell the hunter. Yet many big-game animals have been shot by hunters from the protection of a warming fire in cold weather. Probably the greatest drawback to smoking is that it may draw the game's visual attention to your stand.

But, enough on standing or still hunting.

The best way to get shooting at most big-game animals is through cooperative driving. When man finally first managed to associate with some of his neighbors, he found that group hunting could produce more pounds of game per effort than in going it alone. This varied from setting fires to flush game, driving them over cliffs, or herding them into water to finish them off. Anything which reduced danger to the hunter and produced more meat was deemed justified. It is worth comparison with certain primitive bow hunters who still hunt alone but who use poison on their relatively ineffective arrows to accomplish the same purpose.

Driving game is practiced primarily in the better defined hunting grounds of farm country, where walking in a fairly straight line is possible. Yet, I have participated in drives on the mule deer mesas of Colorado, the antelope river bottoms of Wyoming, and in the heavy forested whitetail country of lower Ontario. All were successful. And, of course, this is a favored method of hunting in my native Pennsylvania and other areas of the East.

In our look at still hunting we covered many of the cautions and recommendations that apply to all types of hunting. For many times there is a thin margin in considering whether a hunter is still hunting or stalking. Even when driving, there are times whan an archer will wait out an animal coming in from the side or trying to sneak back through the drive. Or, he may attempt to stalk one that thinks it is hidden, waiting for the drivers to pass it by.

It should always be kept in mind that a hunt is never over until you are in camp or preparing to enter your conveyance. How many shots are not even taken when an animal wanders toward a group or a couple

Group hunting, or driving, is a successful way to hunt in the more open country.

of hunters who miss the opportunity by loud talking or relaxing too soon? Sometimes it is a late arriving member of the party who unknowingly sends a potential shot opportunity toward his companions.

You are hunting at any time that it is legal to take a shot and you are in hunting territory. Keep alert!

Although there is no reason that driving should not work on all big-game species where terrain and cover permits, it is largely confined to deer hunting. Yet, we have picked up elk in drives; it is not unusual for a bear to come through to the standers or watchers, and various varieties of small game and non-game species such as foxes and coyotes frequently are caught up in organized group hunts. Nevertheless, terrain and the limited numbers of hunters in areas favored by the larger species of game will likely limit driving—as such—for other than deer.

Since we want to take a hard look at all types of hunting for deer—the most sought after big game in most of the states and some parts of Canada—we will skip lightly over driving as a hunting method at this point.

Stalking is by far the most challenging of the methods for taking game with the bow or the gun. It is the most demanding in terms of needed woods lore, patience and knowledge of the game being sought. All the problems of air movement, camouflage, sound and sight are compounded in the average stalk. It starts with sighting the game; it frequently ends with frustration. Even when a perfect stalk has been made, the quarry has often decided to drift away for reasons of its own, or the archer finds that he cannot approach close enough for an effective shot. Or, some other hunter, a farmer, a lumberman, a truck, a low flying airplane, a hidden animal of the same species—any number of factors can foul up a stalk that may have taken literally hours.

A good binocular, always handy in any hunt, is practically a must in planning for a stalk. For, not only must the game be sighted at a distance, all intervening terrain and vegetation must be studied beforehand. It must be considered that there may be long stretches to cover when the quarry will be out of sight. Provisions must be made to reach some specified point from which the stalk can be continued in close proximity to the intended trophy.

Because a stalk usually covers quite some time as well as distance, there may be change in the wind or even the weather. If the animal is reclining in the middle of the day, it will probably remain in the same spot at which it is sighted. But, if it is slowly moving along while feeding, it may move some distance. All of these factors, and more, may work against a successful stalk.

Stalking is by far the most challenging method of hunting any species of big game.

If the animal remains in its bed, trying to get into position for a shot presents the toughest part of the stalk. If it is moving, a bit of still hunting may come into play as you work your way into position to intercept it.

One thing is fairly certain. You must work yourself to a point where you can view the quarry at fairly close range before it sees you.

An animal lying down is a most difficult target. Its position does not offer shots comparable to those usually practiced on paper targets and its legs protect most of its vitals. A low profile from the belly side of a reclining animal leaves you little but the chance of a neck shot. Viewed from the back, you encounter the same shot problems (penetration difficulty) as when shooting from a tree stand. If you can safely toss a pebble to get your quarry on its feet without alarming it into flight, you will have a much better opportunity to shoot.

If the animal is in high weeds or grass, you may have to approach by a belly crawl for hundreds of yards and then make some extremely risky maneuver to get into shooting position. For this reason alone, it is well to have practiced shots from a kneeling position before season opening. But, don't expect your arrow to cut through any extensive grass or weeds and still hold perfect flight. It is still necessary to get a clear shot for much hope of success.

You should have picked out certain markers before making the stalk so as to ascertain when you are getting close to the game. Bumbling in on it at the last moment when you have done everything else right up to that juncture can be most discouraging.

Obviously, such hunting is a solitary venture. You need no help other than your wit, cooperation from the weather and a lot of luck. But it takes skill to score. For the most part, you create your own breaks. And, it takes luck to avoid interference by unrelated elements such as mentioned earlier.

One factor working in your favor is simply that you will be mentally prepared when the proper moment arrives. By the time you get into shooting position, you have been watching your quarry so long that the elements which contribute to nervousness or buck fever have been practically eliminated. Those who can successfully stalk their quarry are seldom those who blow up easily, in any event.

If, as sometimes happens, your intended target has moved into a position that practically precludes a successful shot, don't panic and try to rush in. You have waited this long; wait a little longer. Sooner or later the animal is going to make *some* move. It may, happily, be toward you, so be prepared to permit it to come within shooting range. If it moves in another direction, you will likely be able to continue your stalk.

Another caution. If you started hunting with one or more companions, have an understanding about how and when you are going to get together after going your separate ways. There is little more disheartening than to have some idiot start to beller for you just when you are at the probable end of a successful stalk.

Stalking is possible, of course, only in those areas where the intended quarry can be seen or glassed from a distance. This includes most hunting areas in North America where the terrain is not so flat nor the brush so thick that there is no chance to find your target before you can make a try for it.

But, when you have the opportunity to try, there is no other way of hunting that can give you quite the same feeling of success and exhilaration that stems from winning over the wild.

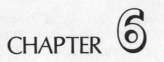

Big Game or Large Game?

Now that we should be pretty well set to go hunting for big game with the bow or the gun, there is possible uncertainty as to whether we are really after *big* or *large* game.

Dictionaries offer little clarification between the two. For example, Webster's Third International Unabridged defines *big* as "large in physical dimensions . . .", and *big game* as "the large animals sought or taken by hunting." And *large* is defined as "exceeding most other things of like kind." The New Century Unabridged says *big* is ". . . large." *Large* is "being of more than common size." *Big game* isn't defined. Webster's New World College Edition calls *big* "of great size", and *big game* as "large wild animals hunted for sport." *Large* is stated as "big as compared with others of its kind."

Unhappily, the dictionaries fail to give us a definition of the in-between species which are neither large nor small when compared to the total zoological zodiac represented by North American wild creatures. Since size has always been the criterion, game such as sheep, goats, pigs and turkeys fall into some sort of a lexical limbo with few words, if any, to categorize them accurately in the hunting scene.

79

Incidentally, the word "quarry", as frequently used in hunting books, has a connotation which goes back to Middle English and comes from the word *querre*, part of the entrails of a beast given to the hunting dogs or, in the case of a bird, to the hunting hawk. And it was also applied to a pile of dead game. Today it is generally used to refer to the object of the chase.

From here on, however, our references to archery tackle mean the maximum that can be handled by the individual bow hunter, and it must be assumed that whatever mentions of quarry are made definitely are written with a genuine big-game species in mind—one that is widely accepted as such by most hunters.

Accepting the bow and its inherent handicaps as a hunting arm, it is necessary to go all the way if we want to deserve the title of sportsman. Neither Boone and Crocket Club membership, the epitome of the gun hunter's ambition in trophy seeking, nor Pope and Young Club, the bow hunter's counterpart, recognize any trophy that was not taken in fair chase. Whether you are interested in posting records with the Pope and Young Club is immaterial for the approach here. However, the rules by which trophies are considered for membership are very much a part of any sportsmanship approach to big-game hunting with the bow. Anything less marks one as merely a hunter—not a sportsman.

Basically, an application to have a trophy considered by Pope and Young Club must have the hunter's signature certifying to the following with a record of the kill:

"Spotting or herding land game from the air, followed by landing in its vicinity for pursuit, shall be deemed UNFAIR CHASE and unsportsmanlike. Herding or pursuing ANY game from motor powered vehicles shall likewise be deemed Unfair Chase and unsportsmanlike.

"I certify that the trophy scored on this chart was taken in Fair Chase as defined above by the Boone & Crockett Club. I certify that it was not taken by spotting or herding from the air followed by landing in its vicinity for pursuit. I further certify that it was not taken by herding or pursuing from motor powered vehicles and that it was taken in full compliance with the game laws of the province or state."

In addition to the copyrighted certification, use of which is permitted Pope and Young Club by Boone and Crockett Club, the archery organization considers a few more points concerning the manner of taking a trophy. Fair Chase is held to *exclude* the following:

1. Helplessness in or because of deep snow.
2. Helpless in water, on ice, or in a trap.

3. While confined behind fences as on game farms, preserves, etc.

4. In defiance of game laws, after legal hours, or out of season.

5. By "Jack Lighting" or shining at night.

6. From a power vehicle or power boat.

7. By the use of any aircraft for herding, driving, landing alongside an animal or herd, or using an aircraft to communicate with or direct a hunter on the ground.

8. By any other method considered by the Board of Directors of Pope and Young Club as unsportsmanlike.

In addition, no aid in the form of tranquilizers, poison, or firearms may be used. No antlers may be measured in velvet or until after a 60-day drying-out period. Some shrinkage will occur, and this insures that everyone is treated fairly since it may be literally years before some entries can be certified by one of the many official measures. All that is necessary for anyone to have a trophy registered, providing that it meets the minimums established for each species, is to get in touch with an official measurer. They are well distributed across the United States. There is no charge for the service, but a recording fee of $10 is required to offset expenses of the nonprofit organization.

For further information about Pope and Young Club, the latest address at this writing is: Douglas Walker, Executive Secretary, Box 1, Squaw Valley, California, 93646.

There are those with the time and money to restrict their hunting efforts to only what might be considered official trophies. By far the vast majority of bow hunters, however, are happy just to score on the particular quarry being hunted. Without belittling in any way the noteworthy accomplishments of Pope and Young, let it be considered right here and now that *any* big-game kill with the bow and arrow under the rules of fair chase is a trophy in which to take pride.

Whether a deer has twelve points or no points is not so important as how it was taken and the limits in opportunity available to the hunter. For example, an outstanding deer was taken by a novice archer some years ago with the fifth arrow. The hit was in the femoral artery which is located in the hind leg. Although this is always a quick kill if the artery is well cut, it is never a desirable target for a discriminating bow hunter. Obviously, if the archer missed the entire deer with four arrows, he couldn't possibly have deliberately hit a pencil-sized target such as the femoral artery. Despite the fact that the hunter received deserved acclaim, as a trophy, circumstances of the kill raise questions.

My first bow trophy was a doe that might have weighed eighty pounds soaking wet. But, she was taken with tackle I made myself, and

Any big game taken under the rules of fair chase is a trophy for the bow hunter.

I hunted her, or the first decent-sized deer that might come along, for years against the guns even before there was a special season for bow hunters. Although there have been some memorable hunting successes both before and since, that little doe will always stand high, if not at the top of anything that has or will ever fall to my bow.

Consider the circumstances of a high-ranking antelope trophy taken at 120 yards. The fellow who took it was certainly risking crippling a magnificent animal. No one of my acquaintances can call his shots at that distance. The same goes for an archer who dropped a forkhorn at 110 yards within minutes of the end of legal shooting hours. Although he dropped the animal on the spot with a lucky neck shot, the arrow could just as easily have taken the deer in the guts. It could have become coyote bait before morning.

From a personal viewpoint, the worst sin in bow hunting is to substitute chance for skill as a hunter, by lobbing arrows at game at ridiculous ranges. Such shooting is more apt to bring criticism to bow hunting than any other fault. It can, and undoubtedly does, produce cripples.

Both the bow and the hunter have limitations. Those who habitually try beyond the reasonable capabilities of each don't belong in bow hunting. Even when we give it everything we have, there will nevertheless be unfortunate instances as in any human endeavor. But, these chance happenings do not preclude adhering to the right or the best principles of sportsmanship in hunting. Every wolf doesn't succeed in downing its quarry even though it may attack its prey and inflict a wound. In my photo file is a picture of a cow caribou standing in a river to cool a hideous wound in her shoulder where presumably a wolf had ripped her unmercifully. A wolf had been heard in the area just before she emerged from the bush. She should have had a calf with her, but none showed, and we could only morbidly contemplate what may have occurred back in the bush. Not every bear, mountain lion, wildcat,

A cow caribou believed to have lost her calf to a marauding wolf. She was injured.

weasel, hawk, owl—(we could go on)—succeeds in killing every victim that feels claws, beak or teeth.

But, since our need is not so great as that of the natural predators, we carry a responsibility to be as mercifully effective as possible in our hunting. We can fulfill this responsibility by acquiring tackle that fits our potential ability and practice until we have a reasonable knowledge of our limitations. Then, we should endeavor to make up for any lack of bow shooting ability with plain hunting ability so that we can get close enough to score cleanly. Anything less is a blot against bow hunting.

In the same vein, there is this business of running shots. They're tough. The relative slowness of an arrow is never more evident than when shooting at running game. This is not to say that a hunter should pass up all running shots when he may have worked hours or days for one particular chance. However, before trying such a shot, he certainly should have practiced them a lot. As to lead, my advice has always been to figure the lead on the running animal that seems about right, then double it before releasing.

A good way to get in some running practice is with an old auto tire and the nearest slope where shooting is practical. Insert a sheet of cardboard inside the tire so that you can mark your hits, then have a companion roll the tire across your shooting line. Your first few arrows are unlikely to produce much more than surprises.

Don't take shots at game running straight away. Your chance of a clean kill is nearly nil. Even on a standing animal, there isn't much to go on unless you want to try for a neck shot. Most times it is best to wait a moment, if possible, for a better angle.

Some time ago there were articles in national magazines recommending by implication, if not by choice, how to kill an animal with a shot between the hind legs and into its vitals or attempting to hit the femoral artery in the hind leg. Both are potentially cruel and unlikely to score.

Those always beautiful, sometimes ferocious creatures over which man has domininon deserve the sportsman's every consideration. If we pursue them in the name of sport, then, damn it, let's play the game in an entirely fair manner that will permit us to savor the triumph as well as the trophy.

CHAPTER 7

The White-Tailed Deer

Although tales of pioneers and Indians are usually inseparable from the buffalo, there is evidence that deer played an even more important historic part than buffalo in the growth of the United States. Because the buffalo emerged as something associated with the depredations of the white men along with the passenger pigeon, it has become a national symbol. And, only because the buffalo, or more properly, the bison, simply can't accommodate to man's greed, he is relegated to zoos and a comparatively few closely managed wild herds.

Not so, the deer.

Despite the unrestricted market hunting in much of the country for many years before the first protective laws were passed, the deer managed to survive wherever there was proper habitat. For, as man ravaged the deer herds, he also killed off the deer's natural enemies, the wolf and the cougar. Meanwhile, from the time the white man set foot in the western world, he began to depend upon the deer to keep him alive and warm. It was estimated that some 54,000,000 pounds of dressed meat, mostly venison, was consumed by Americans in 1942 during a shortage of commercial meat occasioned by World War II. Even today, during periods of meat shortages, venison provides an acceptable substitute for beef.

(Montana Fish and Game photo by Hector LaCasse)

Today hunting for once widespread buffalo is confined to a few private herds.

As the cottontail rabbit is the most sought after species of small game, similarly the deer is the most popular of big-game animals, simply because of its availability in most states. But, the very cleverness of the animal, which insures its survival under proper regulations, makes it also the most challenging of all big-game species. This is particularly true of the white-tailed deer.

Basically, there are only two main species of deer in North America, *Odocoileous virginianus*, the white-tailed deer, and *Odocoileus hemionus*, the black-tailed deer, or mule deer. The mule will be properly recognized in the next chapter. There is some overlap in the ways to hunt each species as well as an overlap in their territories, but each deserves space for those who may only have the opportunity to try for one or the other. The whitetail is to be found on the most widespread basis and consequently is most likely to be the only big-game quarry for the average bow hunter. So he's first.

There are no less than thirty recognized subspecies of the white-tailed deer. Most common is the large northern woodland whitetail which is found throughout northeastern United States. Smaller subspecies are found in the southern states down into Mexico. Only one, Coues whitetailed deer, or the Arizona whitetail or fantail, is recognized as a separate species by Pope and Young Club. So despite minor to major differences in the other 28 subspecies, where hunting is allowed,

The white-tailed deer is the most likely big-game quarry of the average bow hunter.

a whitetail is a whitetail. This, in itself, points up the difficulty in trying to evaluate the true worth of trophies. It is like attempting to lump northern and southern largemouth bass into one class. They don't fit, and separate recognition is today given each.

Those who have hunted both have little trouble distinguishing between a white-tailed deer and the black-tailed, or mule deer. Although young bucks and females are less easily identified, the tail which provides the identifying name, is a dead giveaway. The waving white flag of the whitetail, as the deer trots stiff-legged away or takes great bounds, cannot be mistaken for the seldom-raised black-tipped or black-mantled pride of the mule deer. The ears of the mule deer, which give it its more common name, are also considerably larger than on the whitetail. But unless the two species are side by side, this detail could be missed. However, there is one other characteristic of the mule deer which provides positive identification. When alarmed, the mule deer bounces along almost as though it was mounted on four pogo sticks operating simultaneously. Its flight is somewhat like that of a jackrabbit jouncing above the sage to look ahead when frightened or pursued.

Despite the excellent time a mule deer can make when it goes into its bounce routine—as much as 26 feet at a bound—when extra excited it will run flat out much in the manner of a whitetail. The comparable gait of the whitetail to its black-tailed cousin is a series of bounds, similar to that of horses taking a series of hurdles without changing stride.

Antler development is another almost unmistakable means of identification in mature animals. A white-tailed deer normally has two sweeping branches which drift up and behind the ears before coming forward, the two ends frequently pointed inward toward each other. Points consist of single tines growing up and slightly inward. Occasionally these will have short projections. The brow tines, the first projections from the base of the antlers, are usually better developed in the whitetail.

Mule deer antlers are bifurcated, or dichotomous, meaning that they normally branch, after the single brow tines, into a series of double points, or Y's. Occasionally there will be some similarity in antlers between the two species, but this is regarded as a freakish occurrence and not as something usual. Either species of deer, however, may have some wild arrangement of points other than normal. Such racks, when encountered, are properly classified as nontypical.

Just for the record, all members of the deer family such as moose, elk and caribou, have antlers, not horns. And, they are shed annually no matter how large and permanent they appear. Number of points is not a criterion as to the deer's age in any species. Rather, a big rack simply indicates that the animal is in its prime and that it is enjoying a good diet. In areas of poor food, or food low in the elements which contribute to antler growth, bucks will seldom match antlers with deer ranging more favorable habitat.

Both body size of whitetails and size of their antlers are governed considerably by the availability of food and its type. But, except for the favored few who have the means and time to travel for top trophies, how many bow hunters really concern themselves about size? There are those who will hold out for an antlered deer, but most of these do so in the knowledge that they are going to pick up the gun during the firearms season. Others will try for a big deer, whether it is a buck or a doe. Yet in some of the overpopulated whitetail country, hunters are actually encouraged to take fawns. It is these little fellows that are most apt to starve to death if the winter proves severe. Presumably such a regulation also gets another hunter out of the woods early in areas where the limit is one deer a season. While such a recommendation doesn't stir up much enthusiasm among hunters, the reasoning is valid.

From a hunting standpoint, pre-season scouting for deer is one of

Antler development in the mature whitetail is an unmistakable means of identification.

the best ways to build toward success. Not only do you get to know how, when, and where the animals are moving, you can pick out a specific one to try for in season. This is only practical if you live in or near good whitetail country, of course. And, it can be a waste of time if the area you plan to hunt does not have a special archery season. Once the guns start blasting and the woods are crowded with hunters, the best laid schemes o' deer and men, to paraphrase Bobbie Burns, ". . . gang aft a-gley."

Assuming you will try where there is an archery season, but you have neither the opportunity nor the time to scout a strange area well beforehand, an extra day's look around before the hunt can still mean much. Obviously you are going where there are deer, so give yourself a chance to study the lay of the land before you actually start hunting. If you have been there before, you should know where you will station yourself. It is an empty feeling to start out with the bow in strange territory with no idea of where you are likely to find action.

Deer are creatures of habit. Some hunters fill their license year after year from essentially the same stand. As long as there are no major changes in foilage and terrain, such as lumbering operations or the building of a new highway, deer will continue to utilize the same territory in much the same manner, year after year. Until they are pressed by hunters, they tend to follow the same pattern.

Some of my early bow hunting was done near the top of a saddle in a low mountain range about ten minutes from my coffee pot. I would arrange to be there before daylight even though my deer weren't expected until about an hour later. They would usually appear within a ten-minute span of eight o'clock. Then other hunters began noticing where my car was parked, and I had company.

At 7:45, give or take a minute or two, car doors would slam a few hundred yards below me. Hunters who had to be at work by eight o'clock were leaving. Within a few minutes thereafter, deer would start

Scouting an area before a hunt is valuable if time permits.

working in the direction of my stand. They had drifted in near the cars where there were a couple of old apple trees, and the departing hunters would send them on up the mountain.

Because of the whitetail's habit of following familiar trails, tree stands for hunters have become increasingly popular. Too, the whitetail is most frequently found in forested areas of young growth where it is often so thick that it prefers to follow well-defined trails. There is no question that the elevated stand gives the hunter an advantage relative to scent and sight. This is not to say that a deer will not look up, though. Instinct born thousands of years ago has taught it that its traditional enemies, the big cats, frequently lie in wait on limbs of trees over the trails. However, since its sight is useful mostly only if there is movement or the object evolves into one of its natural enemies, the deer is not likely to become alarmed at seeing the camouflaged figure of a motionless bow hunter.

But tree stands do have their limitations, as mentioned earlier. The archer planning to hunt in this manner has both the practical and moral responsibility to practice shooting from this position.

Those planning to hunt from tree stands should practice shooting from this angle before the season.

It is far better to have the stand, whether it is on the ground or in a tree, to one side of a good runway or trail. This modifies the shot angle to offer a more vulnerable target area and increases the likelihood of a good hit and proper arrow penetration.

The matter of penetration or a pass-through is frequently a subject of some controversy. No experienced bow hunter will dispute the advantage of a low chest hit over any other, but whether it is better for the broadhead to stay in the animal or pass on through raises some question. If the head remains in the animal, it may continue to do the work for which it was designed in the animal's flight. On the other hand, if there is a pass through, there are two orifices to provide a blood trail. In one hit, the shaft, or part of it may remain to keep agitating a blood flow, but the other provides double the bleeding area.

Possibly there is no positive answer to this one. Each hit is certain to be somewhat different. Nevertheless, a blood trail is most desirable since a deer can cover a lot of ground in the time following a mortal arrow wound. This is an important consideration in typical whitetail cover of early autumn.

Driving whitetails is an excellent way to produce shooting. *Taking* deer in this manner is largely dependent upon the experience of those in charge of the drive and the extent of cooperation by the participants. It is best done in familiar country where the probable exits of deer on any particular drive can be anticipated.

There are two generalizations which apply to driving deer. They cannot be driven *far* downwind or downhill. But, this doesn't mean that such drives should not be attempted. It does mean that both probabilities should be taken into consideration.

For example, on a downwind drive the standers, or watchers—or in the West, sitters—are more apt to serve as closed gates through which the deer are unlikely to go. And, if they do attempt to pass through, they will probably be traveling at full speed. Those most likely to get good shooting are the flankers who should start out ahead of the drive and move, if at all, ever so slowly and carefully.

In fact, almost any good drive pattern can be imagined simply by partially spreading the thumbs and forefingers of each hand, and then move one toward the other. This will vary, of course, with terrain. Along a deep river or a high bluff, deer have little choice but to take one of three directions. They rarely take to big water unless really pushed to their limit.

Since deer normally move up toward high points from which they have a choice of direction, drives should be planned with this in mind.

If a brush bottom is being covered, the wooded side should be much better covered than one that is open to fields or thin brush.

But, always, both wind direction and the usual pattern of deer movement must be taken into consideration. This doesn't mean that the direction of the drive is necessarily dictated by such conditions, but the drive should be planned by placing the most bow hunters where action ought to or would seem most likely to occur.

The greatest fault in driving deer for bow hunting is failure to hold down the speed of the drivers. Drivers serve only one purpose—to get the deer moving. Too many, who have switched to the bow from the gun, fail to realize that this is a different ball game. Once a deer is jumped from its bed, the driver has done his job. From that point on he should proceed with the utmost caution. That same deer may scent the standers and sneak back through the drive to provide a driver with a chance shot. You don't want deer to come crashing through unexpectedly.

The second worst mistake is for the standers to move in noisily and flush out deer and alarm others that might have been shoved towards them. There should be absolutely no talking. Standers should be dropped off at favorable spots by hand signals. Remember that the poor guy who is setting up the stand frequently runs out of good spots and may be forced to take the worst of the lot for himself after all his work. The same holds true when setting up the drive. The captain should place his men with the same caution and send his flankers ahead well before the drive gets underway. And timepieces should be synchronized so that everyone moves together.

A third fault is in making the drives too long or too short. This is somewhat governed by the terrain to be covered and the number of hunters, but somewhere between one-half and one mile should do it. On too short a drive, there is too much chance that normal movement of hunters getting into position may move deer out or set them on edge. If the drive is too long, it is difficult to keep it straight or to keep the drivers from crowding up or thinning out too much. This is not difficult later on in the season when the leaves have fallen or snow is on the ground. But it is always tough to maintain the integrity of a deer drive in heavy vegetation.

Of course, the drive isn't over until the captain, or the hunter in charge, says it is. No stander should therefore move until visually contacted or called. The same holds true for the drivers. When they come through, there should be no conversation between drivers and standers. A nod is enough even though there is a great story to tell about the big

Sometimes the captain setting up a drive winds up with no good place to go himself.

one that got away. The big one may be trying to sneak right past the next stander.

Not only can noise spoil someone's chance in a particular drive, it may ruin the next drive before it starts, especially if it is to be in the same area. It is not unusual to cut up a long patch of woodland with several drives.

In unfamiliar or wild country, it may sometimes be advisable to have some form of communication to keep the gang together. We don't want anybody to get lost. In such instances, a light lip whistle may be necessary in driving to keep the line straight. Obviously, it will work against any chance of shooting for the drivers, but this may be preferable to losing someone and fouling up the rest of the day looking for him.

If you have newcomers to the sport or someone who is a stranger to the area, keep them in between two more experienced hunters on both drives and stands. It is quite a responsibility to conduct a deer drive, both from the standpoint of possible success in taking deer and the well-being of the participants.

Drives, of a sort, can be made by even a very few or sometimes merely by two good hunters. Normally, such attempts should be made in relatively familiar territory. It is important that each participant know where he is to go as well as about where the other, or others, should be at any given time. As an example, let's assume that three hunters are going to cover an area from the last bench to the top of a low mountain ridge. Assume the ridge runs from west to east, and a light breeze is moving from the west.

Number One man moves up and out along the top of the ridge, moving rapidly for perhaps ten minutes simply to get into position. The next man moves out along the side, but he stops within five minutes. Then, at a designated time and with timepieces synchronized, all three men start moving ever so slowly, with the third man covering the bench which is now some distance below the other two hunters. They proceed slowly for if the bottom man jumps a deer and doesn't get shooting, it will almost invariably move up the mountain even though at first it may run straight away for a bit. Whitetails will frequently circle under such conditions, and somebody may get a try for it.

Depending upon the time of day, usually late afternoon, a deer jumped on one of the higher trails may head down to get closer to open fields where it plans to feed that evening. Frequently, deer will get out without the knowledge of the man who moves them, but they may move toward one of the other hunters. This is one of the reasons for the emphasis on moving slowly. Deer on the move are alert, but they often make so much noise that they can be heard coming and preparations can be made to get set for a shot.

A variation of the same hunt can be made by dropping one man off upwind and letting him move toward the other hunter or hunters much in the manner of a conventional drive. His scent alone will move deer which will attempt to get around him. Consequently, the other two should be spaced so that they are apt to cross trails with the game.

In such hunting, the idea is to match wits with the deer rather than to force them into movements against their will. This is the greatest problem in driving deer when bow and arrow hunting. Many times the barriers of scent, sound or human movements force deer to take routes not of their choice. Under such conditions they move warily or at high speed, neither of which is conducive to good shooting with the bow. But, if deer are merely nudged from their midday beds or areas of casual browsing, they will pick up their own trails, unalarmed. It is during such moves that the experienced bow hunter has an excellent chance to score. Gun hunters could greatly increase their odds by such hunting. They can cover far more territory with a rifle than the archer who must let the deer come much closer for effective shooting.

In effect, all a deer wants to do when a hunter moseys through its

If deer are not startled, they will pick their own trails, unalarmed.

territory is to move aside and let him pass. It is only when the stealthy hunter gets quite close to a deer, either deliberately or unknowingly, that the deer really spooks. At such times, it may take off at full tilt or get safely out of danger where it can snort and whistle to alarm other game for many yards in all directions.

This alone is reason enough to move slowly and look hard in all directions. The slightest patch of suspicion may actually be a few square inches of a big deer. Check closely before making another move if you can see anything that you cannot positively identify. You can be sure, no matter how good a hunter you are, that you will pass deer successfully depending upon their natural camouflage and immobility to escape your attention.

Try to think like a deer; act like a deer. The deer will be using most of the same tactics you are trying to use if you are hunting properly.

It is not always true that if you can see a deer it can also see you. The trick, however, is to get close enough for a shot before it detects your presence. Frequently, if you see a deer lying down, it has your approach covered even if it hasn't seen you. In such instances, check the air movement, and plan your stalk. If the deer is facing you, chances are that the air is moving from its rear, a common stunt for a smart deer. It means that your stalk must necessarily come from the side, and it should be the side with the best cover.

Even if a deer does see you, it won't necessarily spook. It may just watch for your next move. If you withdraw discreetly, you may be able to approach successfully from another direction. Don't hurry. It will take the deer some time to forget that it saw you and it will be especially wary for a while.

In all hunting, there is probably no greater game than trying to match moves with a white-tailed deer. Stalking. This species has not overcome the need to live practically in man's backyard without acquiring human-associated "smarts" that are probably unmatched by any other wild creature.

Some regard the whitetail buck as a coward because it frequently brings up the rear in a herd of does. This, however, is not unusual for any of the animals which serve under natural conditions as the prey of predators. A deer's only defense is speedy flight. The most dangerous spot is therefore at the rear, not the front of the herd. So, if waiting for a buck, frequently, though not always, the last of a bunch will be one.

Since hunting seasons frequently follow the rut of the deer, the buck's amorous intentions can sometimes be used against him. However, unlike some members of the deer family, he doesn't knock himself out to keep a harem together. Although he will travel with a herd and fight for his rights, he gives his attention to the one or more does in their estrus cycle and doesn't go chasing them all around to keep them in tow. When asserting his sex, he is more inclined to be a bit careless than under normal conditions.

Once, when hunting on a private reserve where the deer are kept wild despite certain limitations on their freedom, I saw a doe come by in a big hurry although there were no other hunters around. She was just walking, but fast. Moments later a nice eight-point came down the identical trail, looking neither right nor left. He was grunting softly with each hurried step. Although he passed within ten yards, I simply didn't have the heart to break up the romance. About an hour later, a six-point that didn't seem to have anything particular on his mind carried my arrow about forty yards before folding up in a creek.

Although deer are basically browsing animals, feeding on twigs, leaves and tender shoots of trees and shrubs, they are also grazers, eating many types of grasses. When browsing in or on the edge of woodland or young growth, their heads are normally somewhat elevated. But since they are in areas of relative security, they are usually then less alert than when out in pasture where there is no cover. Consequently, it is usually easier to stalk a deer in the woods than in the open.

Whether on a drive or a deliberate stalk, using available cover will frequently get you within shooting range. Sometimes it is possible to get a large tree between you and the deer. If you move quietly, watching for any unexpected movement on the deer's part, it is often possible to get quite close. Then comes the problem of getting into position for the shot. If you draw your bow to half strength before exposing yourself and assume a shooting attitude, you may be able to get off a shot before the animal is aware of your presence.

When a whitetail is grazing, its head down in the grass, approaching to shooting position is much more difficult. If there is more than one deer in the field, they seem to take turns lifting their heads for a look around. And, unlike other animals more deliberate in their feeding, a deer will so often drop its head and then bring it up again immediately to catch you off guard. Stalking with more than one deer in the group really complicates the situation.

In such event, it is usually best to work your way to a position ahead of the general feeding direction and simply try to wait the deer out. It is possible to crawl within shooting distance if there is tall grass nearby, but it is still necessary to kneel or stand to shoot. With one deer, it can be done. If there is more than one, it is nigh impossible.

Watch out for fawns. These little devils are extremely nosey and may seek you out if they detect movement. Or, at about the time you are in position, they are apt to snort and alarm the whole herd. Their very fearlessness works against you. Since they may still be varying their vegetarian diet with milk from the doe, they have more time to wander about and look around.

At any time you are making a play for a particular deer, cover the area well for signs of another animal. Does are seldom alone. Most veteran archers have had the exasperating experience of stalking one deer for a long time only to have another snort an alarm. Deer will seldom spook until they are sure of danger, and a hidden deer may watch you make a long stalk before deciding that you are up to no good.

There are times when you suddenly come upon a whitetail that has obviously seen you but hasn't made a move. If you walk obliquely, getting your arrow ready and part draw underway, watching the animal only out of the corner of your eye, you can sometimes stop and get off an arrow before the deer realizes that you have seen it.

This is one of the times when you risk having the deer jump the string, moving out before the arrow arrives. At any time a deer is aware of your presence—and sometimes it doesn't even have to know you are in the same county—it can get out from in front of an arrow completely or move fast enough to cause a bad hit.

There are various theories on why this is so. Some think the deer sees the arrow and ducks it. It is much more likely that the deer hears the twang of the bowstring and takes off. Sound travels at roughly 1100 feet per second; a really fast bow is around 200 feet per second. On a 33-yard shot, it takes the arrow about half a second to arrive. But, the deer has over four-fifths of that half-second to make its move. A whitetail can move out with phenomenal speed starting from a motionless position, particularly if it is alerted.

Anyway, it is unlikely that the deer would associate the arrow with danger even if it could see it. The appearance of an arrow coming straight on would seem no more than the image of a small bird.

When a deer actually appears to lower itself to duck an arrow which passes harmlessly over its back, it is my opinion that the sound—as the arrow passes—makes it *appear* that the deer ducked it when the move was instead actually made *after* the arrow passed. Of course, the angle of an arrow coming at a deer broadside would appear as a somewhat larger image than a straight-on shot. Whatever the answer, we do know that a whitetail can move substantially in a fraction of a second. I know of no other big-game animal with equal capability.

This questions the advisability of releasing an arrow at a whitetailed deer which we know is alerted unless the distance is quite close. The temptation is tremendous regardless of distance. But, an animal at 40 yards in the woods may not be inclined to leave in a rush and perhaps will offer a more favorable opportunity if we wait it out.

Normally, still hunting for deer is a waste of time between the hours of roughly nine a.m. and three p.m. Any movement of whitetails during this period is confined to lazy drifts around their midday bed for sporadic feeding. This is the time that driving pays off since the animals are more concentrated in the deep woods where such hunting is more profitable. But stalking is fine, if you can locate deer before they are aware of your presence.

One of the plus values in driving with a sizable group is in the better recovery rate of mortally wounded animals. It can work the other way if some of the members get excited and immediately take to the trail. The usual, and best way in the event of a hit, is to take no more than three men to work out the trail. No less, preferably more than a half hour should be allowed to pass before anyone goes near the track or blood trail. If the hit is a good one, the deer will be found not far from where it was shot. However, even a mortally wounded animal can be pushed out of the county if the trail is taken up too soon.

Of course, if it is raining, starts raining or snowing, there is no choice but to get after it. Approaching darkness, however, is no reason to hurry the search. In fact, it is all the more reason not to push the animal. Simply mark the spot, return hunting tackle to the car or camp to avoid problems with the law, and then start out after a proper wait. It is quite easy to follow a fresh blood trail by flashlight.

There is considerable difference in trying to recover a deer in the normally heavy brush and woods frequented by the whitetail than in the open areas preferred by the mule deer.

If those attempting to find a wounded deer are unsuccessful or lose the trail, a large group can be a considerable advantage. A drive can be set up in the area where the trail was lost and there is a good chance that someone will find the animal, if dead, or finish it off if it is unable to move well because of its wound.

There is one very important, but apparently little known fact about wounded deer of which all hunters, especially bow hunters, should be aware. Frequently, if a deer is mortally wounded, it will stagger off its intended course just before succumbing to its wound. This is the moment when its heart starts to fail, and the blood trail is likely to end. So many times, where the blood trail ends, the deer lies dead a short distance away.

Plus value in group hunting is in the better recovery rate of mortally wounded animals.

Mark the spot, or have someone remain there, while others work an ever increasing circle from it.

If the blood trail is faint or nonexistent, this is no proof that the deer is not badly wounded. Hemorrhaging may all be internal. But, if there is evidence at all, and the deer still cannot be found, narrow your search around the nearest water. Almost invariably a wounded deer will seek water in short order if it is able to move. Above all, don't wander around aimlessly looking for it. Think. Try to think like a wounded deer.

In the normally dense cover favored by the white-tailed deer, morning hunts are best. There is the remainder of the day to trail a wounded animal; there is plenty of time to get a carcass out of the woods; deer are easier to take when they are moving to their more secure coverts after a night of foraging. But, whenever or wherever you take a whitetail with the bow and arrow, you have bested the cleverest big-game animal in North America.

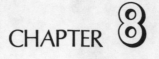

Mule Deer

Those familiar with the somewhat crowded and close-range whitetail deer hunting of the East will find mule deer hunting a wide open pleasure. The muley is frequently found in consort with the jackrabbit in places where the Eastern whitetail would run himself to death trying to find a place to hide. Although whitetails are also found over much of the mule deer range, this chapter will be confined to hunting the black-tailed Westerner. Hunting whitetails, of course, is much the same wherever they are found.

Except in the Northwest, whitetails are more or less incidental to some areas and ranges. Where they do occur, they follow somewhat the same pattern that they do in the East, seeking heavy cover on the slopes and mountains or stream-bordered thickets. The exceptions are in New Mexico and Texas. Southern whitetails are the Coues whitetailed deer.

The basic animal discussed here is the Rocky Mountain mule deer, *Odocoileus heminous heminous*. Like the whitetail, the mule deer has a number of close cousins, eleven in all. Only one, the Columbian black-tail is recognized as a separate species by the Boone and Crockett Club. However, the Sitka deer joins its close Columbian cousin on the northern shores of British Columbia and southern coastal Alaska. The two are collectively known as the coast black-tailed deer. Despite some hybridization between the coastal and inland mule deer, biologists believe that the so-called blacktail is gradually emerging as a completely different species of deer.

Frequently, an Easterner's first good view of the mule deer comes as a surprise for he may have been looking at the animal for some time without even being aware of its presence. The ability of a muley to blend into its natural surroundings is an amazing fact of Nature. It takes some time before a hunter unaccustomed to the West can make out the camouflaged form of a mule deer even though it may be completely exposed to view.

This should be a strong hint that a good pair of binoculars is essential hunting equipment in mule deer country. Another surprise awaiting the uninitiated who comes from the East is the difficulty in judging distance. In heavily thicketed Eastern forests, it is quite common to overshoot deer with the bow and arrow since they are often much closer than they appear to be. In the open areas of the West, sometimes

Black-tailed deer in California.

almost completely devoid of vegetation, game frequently appears much closer than it really is. The tendency is to undershoot or to take shots beyond the hunter's ability simply because they appear much closer than their actual distance.

When choosing a binocular, it is important that it be one which can be carried tucked inside the shirt or a large pocket. Otherwise, there is always the risk of catching the optics with the bowstring or fouling up the draw when the bulge or the actual binocular gets in the way. There is little more disturbing than having any object oscillate from one's neck or shoulder when hunting with the bow and arrow.

My muley hunting with the bow and with the camera has been confined primarily to California, Colorado, Wyoming and South Dakota. Personal experience has quashed for me two common fallacies common to eastern hunters. The first, and one that is sometimes shared by gunners from wide areas who have hunted both the whitetail and the mule deer, is that the muley is stupid by comparison with the whitetail. The other is that mule deer run substantially larger than Northeastern whitetailed deer.

All animals have limited intelligence when compared with human understanding. If this is not true, the horrendous highway kill of animals would not occur. Even when we are trying to build up our own ego through citing the great cunning of our quarry, we are forced to admit to the limitations in intelligence possessed by dumb animals as compared to that of the human.

It is a personal feeling that the whitetail and the muley are about equal in intelligence. True, anyone who has hunted the mule deer is aware of its habit of running off a ways and then turning to stare back at its pursuer. This is more a matter of instinct than stupidity or intelligence. The deer is simply trying to figure out what you are going to do next, and it has never quite figured out the effectiveness of a firearm. But, it has been hunted with the bow for countless thousands of years. If you were a wolf, or a bear, or a cougar, deer would know what move to make after *you* made *your* move. Its normal stop helps protect it against things such as bows and predators.

Although it is not so obvious, the whitetail does about the same thing. This is more apparent to archers since they very often are unable or do not wish to shoot just as a whitetail jumps up in front of them. Quite often the whitetail will run off a bit and then turn around to study the situation, much as does a mule deer. The whitetail is usually protected and often hidden by trees or brush. The mule deer simply adds more distance in the belief that its fleetness of foot will give it the edge it needs if it is pursued. Instinct teaches it that it will be pursued at whatever speed its adversary can move. It has not learned much about ballistics. But, at the distance where it makes its distinctive stop to decide on its next move, it is usually well beyond sensible bow range.

As with the whitetail, the biggest mule deer bucks are the most canny. They get big by being smarter than others of their kind. Really big bucks are more apt to travel alone than with a herd. The exception, of course, is when a number of does in any given herd are nearing or in their estrus period.

When it comes to weight, mule deer rate somewhat with the whitetail. Their generally larger antlers tend to make the Western deer appear considerably bigger although statistics indicate that both the whitetail and the mule deer range in size according to their habitat. The Rocky Mountain mule deer, most common and largest of the black-tailed deer, will go up to about 380 pounds. However, the average is considerably less than that, averaging about the same as the Eastern whitetail. Pennsylvania whitetails average out, field-dressed, at about 125 pounds. Yet in New Hampshire, studies have shown that early season deer have averaged about 192 pounds. The State of Maine reports numerous deer

When the muley makes its distinctive stop, it is usually beyond sensible bow range.

in the 300-pound class. It would appear that, under ideal conditions, the biggest Rocky Mountain mule deer would have a slight edge in weight over the biggest whitetails.

Under today's conditions, however, there appears to be little difference if an average were taken of all whitetails and mule deer taken by hunters.

In all states which provide an early season for bow hunters, there are a couple additional advantages. Deer are considerably larger as they enter the rutting period than after their amorous intentions have subsided early in winter. Bucks can lose up to nearly one-fourth of their body weight by the end of the rutting period. Part of this stems from their extra activity in chasing does. However, all male deer tend to go off their feed during this period and naturally lose weight.

Another lesser advantage is the fact that before deer put on their winter coats, arrow penetration is a bit easier. There is an amazing difference between the heavy, buoyant hair which prepares the animal for the cold months, and the lighter summer pelage.

It is normal to find heavier archery tackle in use by Western hunters. This appears to be a trend more than a necessity, however. Although it is my belief that nothing under 40 pounds at the archer's draw should be used for deer, it is the old and true story that the bow hunter should use the heaviest tackle that he can shoot well. It is probable that those who are less closely associated with organized archery, where knowledge is better developed and utilized, carry bows well in excess of the 50-pound class for deer.

Western hunters, according to my personal observations, carry about 10 pounds more bow weight than their Eastern counterparts. There is no indication that Westerners are any stronger or better developed physically since many of them have moved from the East. It is possible that the more open hunting invites longer shots. In the event of a hit, it is much easier to follow a wounded deer on the average Western terrain than it is on the leaf-covered forest floor or in the thick weed patches of the East.

Of the various methods used in deer hunting, stalking the deer is much more practiced in mule deer country. Here is where a good binocular comes into play. In canyon country, it is frequently possible to glass hundreds of almost vegetation-free acres looking for a telltale patch of hair, antlers, or movement of game. Once an animal is located, depending upon air movement, a stalk may mean literally miles of walking to get into position. At other times, deer may luckily be seen quite close to the hunter's location. In the more arid or open regions, mule deer will take advantage of any shade during the day. This is frequently a wind-carved hollow just beneath a canyon rim, or it may be a veritable sandstone nest beneath large projections of stone. And, they may permit you to come quite close.

Mule deer seem more sensitive to noise than the whitetail. This is probably because in the big country of the West there are far fewer ordinary sounds such as those associated with the much more heavily populated areas of the East.

And, when a muley finally loses his nerve, he is much more apt to go streaking from his bed than to stand and survey the situation if some sound has disturbed him. Often there is little or no cover to hide his retreat. He instinctively knows that others of his kind are bedded down at the same time. Even if the sound might be coming from another deer, the big-eared Westerner undoubtedly suspects that that deer has been moved by something that disturbed it, something dangerous to his safety. Consequently, any stalk made on mule deer must necessarily bring into play the utmost stealth and care.

Driving of a sort is quite possible and can be productive in the canyons even with only a few hunters. Where possible, one man can be sent to the bottom of the canyon with two or more companions flanking the top edges. Flankers should be well on ahead since the deer will usually head for the high spots even though they may run for some distance in a straight line. Biggest difficulty for the flankers is the fre-

Use of a binocular sometimes locates deer that might be missed with the naked eye.

quently broken edges of canyons with their many side ravines and canyon fingers. Each of these should be thoroughly studied before they are entered since they are favorite bedding spots for mule deer.

If the pattern of deer movement through canyons to feeding or watering spots is known, it is not difficult to find a natural blind of stone or brush. If the movement is somewhat indiscriminate and deer tend to fan out over a wide area in their movements, it may be necessary to build a blind of sage or some other handy vegetation.

I recall one particularly discouraging week in which my oldest son built a blind of sage after observing the usual pattern of numerous mule deer movements through a shallow basin leading into a large canyon. The deer crossed the basin each morning, but rather than go into the canyon, they would move up on the prairie toward some other destination. For several days they had passed a given point, and that is where he established his blind. He had numerous chances at does, but the bucks that normally came through were avoiding the spot. Consequently, on the last morning, he moved to the opposite side of the basin which seemed to be favored by the antlered deer. Of course, that morning six bucks milled about his former blind while he watched helplessly out of range.

When deer hunting in the high mesa country, prior to the game's being pushed down by snow, driving is much more practical than in the open prairies and canyon country. Areas of quaking aspen or scrub oak provide driving opportunities quite similar to those in Eastern forests. But, because there is so much territory to hunt, Western drives are frequently quite long and cover considerably more area. If a probable movement of alarmed deer is known, excellent stands can be established for those on the waiting end of the drive. Despite the larger areas to cover, terrain is frequently such that deer can be funneled through the more obvious spots such as heads of canyons and necks of timber created by open areas of stone or sand. In such areas, having someone along with knowledge of the terrain and deer habits is essential for any consistent success.

An exception to this is along river bottoms where there are frequently stands of cottonwood trees and thickets of young quaking aspen. Careful driving in such cover can produce good shooting. A too hurried drive may send the deer into the surrounding hills and canyons. But, if care is used, the game will stick to this cover or briefly take to the outside to permit the drivers to pass before returning. Other times, they may break into the open to gain ground and return to the thicket ahead of the drivers. Of course, their purpose in breaking away may be

Western drives are sometimes quite long, requiring the use of off-the-road vehicles.

simply to cut behind the drive so that they can resume whatever it was they had in mind before being disturbed.

As in any deer hunting with the bow, stealthy movements and the slow approach, with frequent stops, are much preferred over a headlong rush toward the standers. The mule deer habit of stopping to reconnoiter after it has jumped from its midday bed works to the advantage of any other drivers in the area. And, it is certainly true that many deer are moved out by drivers without their knowledge. These may work toward another driver as well as toward the waiting standers, or sitters.

The term *sitters* created an unimpressive connotation in my mind the first time I heard it since I had always advised the standers to keep alert on drives in the East. That was before I made my first stand at the head of a canyon in Colorado where I could look over the Colorado River into Utah. It was well over two hours from the time the drive started until the first driver could be seen in the distance descending the canyon in front of me. But, the drivers knew what they were doing. Deer came bursting out of the canyon a short time later like so many sparks from a short circuit. Since I was trophy hunting, I elected to pass up a nice two-by-three for the dubious privilege of missing a little forkhorn in a desperation try on the very last day of my hunt.

Proof that mule deer can be driven was certainly illustrated on that hunt. The first day of driving we counted 16 bucks and 54 does. The second day produced twenty antlered deer and fifty females.

In a comparison of mule deer and whitetailed deer—and comparisons are natural for anyone who has hunted each—I find little difference in arrow effectiveness. By the same token, the methods of following up a hit are no different for either deer.

Although the muley may stand around longer than the whitetail, it is apt to travel much farther distances to a position of relative safety once it takes off. This is reason enough to delay looking for a deer which has been hit. While it is true that it may be easier to spot an animal downed by an arrow, this advantage should not be negated by moving in too soon before the arrow has had a chance to do its work. In the East there is usually a road or a good trail within a reasonable distance of any kill. In the West, terrain may be such that it is impossible to get even an off-the-road vehicle anywhere near the spot where the animal succumbs. Consequently, pushing a wounded animal to the limit of its endurance can make a lot of trouble for the hunter even if he is successful in finding a deer. It is a natural tendency for any animal which is mortally wounded to go into the most inaccessible area possible to escape its pursuer. Trying to drag or carry a deer out of some of the mule deer country can be a back-breaking sequel to a thrilling experience.

In total, it has been my experience that aside from differences in

Big country sometimes requires long drives.

terrain and climate, hunting mule deer and whitetails require much the same preparation, woods lore and tackle.

There are few advantages to the hunter between the two species. Because hunting territory is frequently much more open, it is possible to see more game in mule deer country and to make plans accordingly. It is just as true that the trophy bucks are tougher to come by since they tend to be solitary, particularly in the early part of the season when special privileges are provided for bow hunters. One real advantage accrues to the mule deer hunter in that the animal is less apt to jump the string than the wary whitetail. In all the shots I have taken at mule deer, if the animal was not already moving, it stood for the shot. Not so the whitetail.

One other caution is in order for the Easterner seeking mule deer for the first time. Antlers are generally much larger, but *trophy* heads are comparably larger. Particularly when they are in the velvet, which is common in the early season in the West, and what is considered a modest rack by Western standards may appear huge to the Easterner. Of course, this is a matter of individual selection, but you may end up empty-handed if you continue to hold out for a big one. Any deer with the bow is a trophy for my money, and those who travel long distances for their hunt at considerable expense may wish to bring home at least some evidence of their excursion.

Above my desk is the head of an eastern Wyoming muley that gave

When in the velvet, mule deer antlers appear larger than they are, but this is a good one.

me a special thrill and just may have been trying to even the score. On a running shot, I had sent an arrow through both hind legs and the broadhead severed the hamstring on the left. After considerable tracking, I finally cornered the big four by four where he had taken refuge up a side draw, under a large, flat stone.

"Be careful, he may be on the prod," my guide warned me.

Since the buck was lying down, legs toward me at eye level, I tried for a neck shot. The arrow caught him in the right shoulder, a poor hit.

The old boy came right out of his bed straight toward me where I was hanging to the dirt side of the canyon. For an instant, I didn't know whether to try for up or down. But the deer turned before it reached me, and I slammed another arrow into it. My buck went around the corner and disappeared beyond another big dirt projection along the side of the canyon.

Of course, there is no way of knowing whether the deer was actually attacking. But it had plenty of room to go, other than at me, including down and out the bottom into the canyon. I moved carefully around the point, an arrow nocked and ready.

Again the buck had taken refuge under a large, flat stone; again its legs protected its vitals at eye level. The guide had moved in above the deer.

"Can you get him on his feet," I urged. "I can't get a good shot from this position."

The guide tossed small stones and dirt clods at the animal, but it refused to budge. I was anxious to finalize the event.

"Stand back, and I'll try another neck shot," I told him.

The distance was closer this time, perhaps fifteen yards. My shot was good, and immediately blood began to well from the wound. Almost as soon, the buck lunged to its feet, sending the guide scrambling up the side of the canyon, and again the deer came straight for me. But it was having trouble finding purchase on the steep dirt side with its hind feet, and I stood my ground. Suddenly the deer's feet went out from under it, and it slid some twenty feet to the bottom of the draw. It was all over.

This was only the second time in my life while hunting that I had been challenged by a wild animal. I still don't know for certain whether the deer would have tried to impale me on the eight needle points coming my way. But in view of the fact that the animal was badly wounded, and it had much better directions to take, it would seem that it had at least some malicious and righteous intent.

Wyoming muley that challenged me after hectic chase.

A friend told me of a similar instance with a mule deer that was down by the hind quarters. Despite its incapacity, it lunged after a hunter and came within a hair of jabbing its antlers into him when he fell trying to escape.

My unarmed guide was raised in mule deer country, and he made a discreet retreat when my deer apparently charged. I am forced to conclude that if it wasn't a bona fide attack, it was a right good simulation.

Incidentally, however unfortunate the delay in killing this buck, it did provide a revealing though unintended field demonstration. Two of the arrows hit when the animal was completely motionless. Although there was a quick reaction, there was still an instant before the animal moved. It didn't even twitch when the arrows struck, as though it was completely unmindful of them. I saw a similar reaction, evidence of lack of pain or discomfort, when I finished off a wounded caribou once with an arrow for a gunner who had run out of ammunition.

Although certainly not enough experience to draw a firm conclusion, these happenings *seem* to support the premise that an animal

Cloth bag is used to protect deer carcass from flies in early season hunt.

seldom feels any initial pain or discomfort from arrow penetration. But fortunately, all other big-game animals I have taken were dead when I moved in for recovery.

Whatever opinions others might have in comparing the white-tailed deer and the mule deer as quarry for the bow hunter, I have the greatest respect for this Westerner. Furthermore, I concede it a notch above the whitetail at the dinner table.

As the muley buck stands against the side of a canyon or all but melts into the shelter of an aspen stand, it is a stately and imposing creature that for the average bow hunter will forever be a challenge in the West.

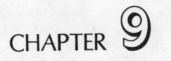

CHAPTER 9

The Bears

In all the years I have hunted, almost without exception the quarry took flight the instant it identified me as a human. The "almost" provided two of the most thrilling episodes in my experience. One involved a bear. The other was an encounter with a mule deer (Chapter 8).

In total, over a period of years prior to the bear encounter, I had spent five different weeks in Maine, Ontario and Quebec suffering the stench, the black flies and the mosquitoes associated with hunting bear over baits. The nearest I had come to a shot was the sight of a little fellow bouncing back into the brush as we rounded a turn on an Ontario road. Then, one evening it seemed that I had hit pay dirt on the sixth try.

Art Scott had dropped me off near a bait on his lease above Mont Laurier, Quebec, in late afternoon after we had previously freshened the pile of scrap meat. On the first trip, we had also cut an opening in the brush to provide a stand about thirty yards from the pile. However, on my return, the breeze had shifted. I hurriedly cut a new opening on an old bear trail. It placed me closer to the bait than I liked, but my station was well hidden.

It was the usual wait, livened only by the visible drumming of a grouse through a hole in the leaves. At sunset, I heard a sound from above the bait, near a close scattering of huge boulders, that sounded like something chewing on a bunch of twigs. Then I heard a cough. Circumstantial evidence was strong, but no bear showed. It was past time to shoot, but I waited a bit longer in hopes of finally just seeing a bear.

There was no further sound and no movement. At last I tiptoed to the edge of the bait and looked up toward the boulders, still bent at the waist to peek under the overhanging brush.

Those familiar with the out-of-doors know that there is a moment in the woods each evening when everything of a dark color turns completely black. It was that time. And yet, I thought I saw the outline of a bear, a big bear. It appeared to be standing upright, its body pointed ninety degrees to my position, its right paw resting on one of the boulders, its head turned my way.

Since I had already made up my mind not to attempt a shot in the fast waning light, I just stared at the apparent apparition, trying to put life into it. My mind wavered between belief and disbelief. It actually looked too big to be a bear. But, since whatever it was appeared to be looking at me, and black bears are (presumably) afraid of humans, I decided my eyes were playing tricks.

So, I stepped to the edge of the wide pile of fifteen years' accumulation and stood erect, still facing the boulders. My "bear" didn't move. After all that, I was finally convinced that it truly was an apparition, so I was about to leave.

Suddenly, the thing let out a loud, "Waaangh."

It was a nasty, belligerent challenge with only the hint of a question mark. And still it didn't move. My bear had materialized!

I decided it was time for somebody to move. I was actually more apprehensive than scared. My bow was at the ready, but it would be of no immediate value if the bear charged. Anyway, the big fellow could be on me before I could get to full draw. I measured the distance the next day at seventeen yards.

Slowly, I took a step backward. Then another. A third.

At completion of the third step, the bear dropped down to all fours and disappeared. I discovered later in daylight that there was an excellent trail among those shoulder-high boulders that I had missed on my first trip. When I reached the nearby, alder-arched log road, the light was better. I walked the several hundred yards to the main dirt road—fast!

This experience points up and to some degree confirms that black bears are seldom dangerous. I firmly believe that my bear, with his poor eyesight, possibly thought I was another bear in my hunched over position when I was first visible to him. When I stepped to the edge of the bait, erect, he became confused. He let out a challenge to warn me that it was *his* bait, whatever I was. Then, when I backed off, he decided that I was a *people*. That made up his mind, and he finally did what black bears are supposed to do when they see humans. However, I can't discount the fact that he didn't scurry away; he simply dropped to all fours and disappeared among the rocks. He didn't appear frightened.

From the bears I have seen, under other circumstances and in zoos, my friend must have been in the neighborhood of five hundred pounds. In subsequent conversations with the outfitter, it came out that a woman had recently missed two shots with a rifle at a bear on that same bait. From her description, it would have had to be at least a thousand-pounder. Impossible, of course, for black bears rarely go over six hundred pounds. But, he was big!

Whether or not an attempt to shoot would have brought on a charge, I'll never know. The bear was obviously agitated. I am convinced that it was still a bit uncertain as to my identity. But, even discounting this possibility, I wouldn't risk merely wounding so magnificent a creature in the uncertain light. I tried again the next afternoon, but my bear didn't come back.

Two days before, my son—who bears my same name but who also answers to Chip—killed a bear that he had nicked with an arrow the previous evening.

Chip had been interrupted packing for the trip by a telephone call, and he had left some of the hardware for his bow on the telephone stand at home. Fortunately, I had an extra bow along, and he put in some practice the first day before taking a stand over a fresh bait. He came back to camp understandably excited, with a handful of bear fur. His only worry was that he might have only wounded the animal since he couldn't find his arrow. We made a midnight trip back to his stand in an unsuccessful attempt to find either blood, bear, or both.

In the better light of morning, he found his unbloodied arrow. Chip felt better. That afternoon he endured black flies and mosquitoes on the same stand while big trout splashed temptingly in the lake nearby. A bear came in and finally offered a maybe shot through a hole in the brush. Chip was sure of a hit. And, he thought he heard the bear moan after it had ripped a path back into the heavy bush from which it came. It would have been foolhardy, however, to go into the bush without help in the little remaining light.

His confidence in having made a good hit was confirmed the next morning when his bear was found no more than forty yards from where he shot it. The arrow had gone through both lungs and the heart to emerge completely on the opposite side.

The possibility struck me, as the bear was being unloaded from the canoe at the dock, that it might have been the same one he had nicked the evening before. Sure enough, a check revealed where his previous arrow had just broken the skin behind the shoulder, without actually slicing through the hide.

After the torture of spring bear hunting over baits, I finally killed my first bear as an adjunct to a moose hunt, again at Arthur Scott's Quebec hot spot. It was only a small yearling sow, but it had the beautiful pelt that develops in the fall before bears head for winter bedding.

This points up an advantage that the bear hunter has in moose country. Most outfitters don't want unnecessary shots taken with a gun during the moose season to avoid stirring up the more favored quarry. But since a bow is silent, it does not adversely affect the main hunting.

Actually, I had walked some ten miles that morning up and down a nearby mountain to a couple of good moose marshes. Since there had been reports of a bear hitting the disposal area behind camp, I decided to lay for it—literally. I awoke from an intended nap near a good bear trail to find what appeared to be about a two hundred and fifty pound

Chip returns with black bear that didn't learn its lesson.

blackie heading diagonally in my direction. It was moving in cautiously, a few steps at a time interspersed with careful sniffing of the faint breeze. Although I was wearing a red camouflage suit, the bear looked my way numerous times with no particular agitation. Then I felt a breeze against the back of my neck. I could almost see my scent go towards the bear. It had one front foot on a stump to get a better snootful, then it dropped down and waddled unhurriedly back into the bush toward a nearby swamp.

As I climbed to my feet, I realized that it would have been impossible to get into position for a shot without being detected. But in the hope that the bear might return, I took a position behind a tree, its trunk perhaps six inches in diameter. Within ten minutes, a bear approached from a slightly lower angle. I picked a clear spot just past a knee-high rock for my shot. Again, it was a case of the bear moving a few feet at a time between time outs to sniff the air and look over the area.

The bear stopped behind the rock. However, since I could see its full chest, I aimed carefully and released. There was a "thock", as though the arrow might have hit a tree, and the bear rocketed back toward the swamp. It seemed to be running with a low profile.

A search at first revealed neither blood nor arrow. But then, at a spot farther beyond, twenty-seven yards from my stand, there was good blood sign. I placed my bow against a bush and went back to camp to sweat out the hit. After fifty minutes, Art—my Indian guide—and I took up the trail. Art carried a gun with the promise not to use it unless absolutely necessary.

We found the dead bear with no trouble about eighty yards from where it had been hit. The aluminum arrow was still in the cervical vertebrae. That bear had carried its head with muscle power alone since its neck was badly broken. It was not the bear I had first seen, but a yearling, probably still traveling with its mother.

These examples are given because I am convinced that this is one of the most sporting ways to take bears with the bow. However, there are some important general points about hunting black bears since their nature doesn't vary much even though habitat usually dictates their activities.

As with any big-game animal, black bears can be stalked under the right circumstances. In spring, bears reveal themselves to eat grass, apparently to sweeten their stomachs after the big sleep and to add needed nutrients. But, bear hunting purely in a grassy area is too uncertain since this food is easy to come by in most bear country. In coastal

Art Scott checks blood sign on leaf where my bear hesitated long enough for a shot.

inlets and bays, bears feed in spring and fall. But, except for areas of Alaska and the Northwest, there is little coastal hunting. In late summer they may be found on hillsides picking berries. Summer bears, depending upon how early or late the season, are apt to have poor pelts.

So for the most part, bow hunters have a choice of taking bears only with dogs or over bait. Even the bear I took in Quebec, although we had not baited for it, was intercepted on its way to a camp disposal area.

In most situations, when bears are taken with dogs, they are shot out of trees. However much writers may play up the sometimes strenuous exercise associated with keeping within baying distance of the dogs, the coup de grace in those situations is a form of glorified target practice. The bear has no real choice. If the archer misses, he has additional chances even though it may be necessary for the dogs to put the bear up another tree.

There are even some places where you can buy a guaranteed hunt. Bears are baited into live traps and held until the unsuspecting hunter comes along. Then the animal is released, the hunting party is steered that way, and within a short time the bear is treed by the dogs.

Black bears have notoriously poor eyesight. However, there appears to be nothing wrong with their hearing or their sense of smell. Consequently, stalking is usually done in the more remote areas where the game's fear and knowledge of humans is less developed. In some of the better bear country, where the animals are hunted by both bowmen and gunners, they are extremely wary. In Pennsylvania, for example, with a population of about 250 people to the square mile, the annual bear kill by gun hunters runs from a low of about 250 to over 600. Compare this with the population of Maine, another good bear state, population about 30 to the square mile. Or Oregon, with perhaps 19 people to the square mile.

Since neither baiting nor the use of dogs are permitted in Pennsylvania, only one bear has been recorded as taken by an archer according to the records of the Pennsylvania Archery Association. That one was shot by Lester H. Newell in Forest County, during the gunning season

My bear was only a yearling sow, but it had the beautiful pelt acquired in autumn.

in 1944. From a private source, I learned of one other, but illegal kill.

This points up the difficulty of taking a bear with a bow in the more heavily populated states by stalking. As in all big game hunting, stalking is the most sporting method. But it is nigh impossible except in those areas previously noted. However, let's take a look at what is required to move in on and kill a blackie with a bow.

In Alaska, you have the best chance during the spring season when the bears investigate the shoreline for dead creatures tossed up by the waves and feed on the lush grass. In fall, bears follow the salmon runs. At such times there is good stalking from the bush trails and big boulders along the beach. In the fall, stalking bears in the blueberry bushes after glassing them from afar can also be a challenging pursuit.

But, whether stalking bears that are following natural food or waiting them out near man-provided bait or on their trails to the bait, the hunter faces much the same problems.

As with all game, the necessity to remain motionless when under their scrutiny is paramount. You may be heard, you may be scented, you may be seen. But, until your movement associates you with the alert provided through the animal's senses, you might just possibly be ignored for the moment.

A bear which will come in to a bait—which certainly retains some

A typical bear bait with meat and bones scattered over a wide area by feeding bruins.

human odor if it was placed but hours before—is accepting a certain risk. It has fed safely before on such bait. Art Scott starts placing bait by snowmobile, and early bears certainly pick up human scent. Sherwood Schoch, professional archer and former editor of *Archery World Magazine*, shot a bear over a bait in Maine that had been placed no more than but twenty minutes before. I know, because I helped place the bait! We rattled cans and made plenty of noise before leaving in a truck to let any listening bear know that now the coast was clear. It wasn't, of course.

Bears are alert to sound. But there undoubtedly are sounds which are aurally investigated many times during the day and night. As long as they don't persist long enough to alarm the creature, it will wait a proper time and move along.

Visually, you have an edge on the bear. Keeping in mind that it is a predatory creature with best forward vision, plan your moves when the animal's head is turned from you. Certainly full camouflage will work in your favor although it is probably less essential than when hunting animals better rated by oculists.

Okay. The preceding should give you an edge on the bear. But, you might as well know it; a bear may have made a complete circle of your stand before chancing an appearance. If you have moved at the wrong time, or you don't smell right, or you are being careless with your can of bug repellent, you may never see the bear that really wants to join you near the bait.

You already know my general feelings about tree stands; they don't vary with respect to bear hunting. In fact, because baits are generally placed on the edge of heavy bush or swamps, a good blood trail is even more essential than in some other types of bow hunting. If you're afraid, I suggest you stick to the gun because, if you are no better shot than I am at unknown distances, you want to be very close to your target. I like twenty yards; prefer fifteen. It is rare to get a second shot; that first one must count.

One of the most knowledgeable bear hunters I've met guided some of us at Harold Schmidt's Wapiti Camp near the foot of Mount Katahdin on the edge of Baxter State Park in the State of Maine. Ernest Shaw, one-fourth Penobscot Indian on his dad's side and a third Passamaquoddy on his mother's, claimed over four hundred bears trapped and shot.

Shaw trapped back when there was a $25 bounty, later reduced to $20, then $10. Today, of course, the bear is a recognized game animal. Ernest told us that a big boar bear has about eight quarts of guts and

Tree stands for bear hunting have same advantages and disadvantages as when hunting deer.

eight quarts of blood. Yet, Harold, who is the only outfitter I know who has shot a bear with the bow, claims that his recovery rate is better on bears shot with an arrow than on those which don't drop to bullet wounds. A bear will bleed heavily from an arrow which will soon cause death. It is not as frightened as one shot with a gun, and it may not be in as big a hurry to get out of the country. Of course, the gun is much more apt to upend the blackie on the spot.

According to Ernest, a black bear must first discharge a greasy rectal plug upon leaving its winter bed and before starting to feed. Even then, it will eat no more than a half-pound to two pounds at a feeding. But, it may cover many miles to find skunk cabbage, mushrooms, carrion, berries, beetles and any other edibles. Sometimes a bear may visit rotted meat merely to lick up the carrion beetles which soon cover such bait.

One thing seems fairly certain. Bears won't be found far from a good water supply since they require ten to twelve quarts a day. A sow with cubs is less apt to be found around a bait since she avoids the more aggressive boars. Boars will kill the cubs if given the chance although a smaller sow will normally knock hell out of a boar twice her size. Ernest believes that any cuttings around a bait should have the fresh cut covered over with mud. This advice is probably a holdover from his trapping days, but I don't believe you can afford to ignore anything which might help your chances.

Although the best chance for success is with an outfitter who is in the business of baiting bears for his customers, you can go it alone in good bear country. Trash fish make a good attraction if you can obtain a ready supply, but they don't hold up well and must be replaced almost daily, depending upon the weather.

Hunting is sometimes permitted at municipal dumps in bear country, but you may invite the wrath of the nearby populace. Bears become sort of adopted pets at such spots. However, at some northern lumber camps you may be welcomed, depending upon how much of a nuisance the bears may be making out of themselves. Orchardists welcome bear hunters since blackies not only love to gorge on fruit, especially apples, but they damage trees with their ponderous weight trying to get at the fruit. Eating bark, particularly where more natural food is scarce, can also make black bears unwelcome.

In any event, when a bear shows itself, try to believe that it is likely to be much more afraid of you than vice versa. Move ever so carefully to get into position for the shot, most preferably when the bear is broadside so that you can try for the heart. Release, then freeze. If your shot is good, the bear will take off. If it comes in your direction, it is likely proof that it hasn't seen you. It may not go far before pausing to lick its wound. Move, and you may frighten it into the next county or invite it to take a swipe at you as it goes by.

This is reason enough to make your stand in a position to the side of the nearest bear trail. Old bait sites usually have definite trails leading to them. Your bear will take the nearest exit. At least I think it will.

So, you take a couple or three black bears and decide that you are ready for a grizzly, the silvertip hunchback of British Columbia and thereabouts, or its cousin, the behemoth brown bear of Alaska. Or, if legal, a Polar bear. Well, sir, you didn't read Saxton Pope closely enough. The first grizzly he encountered in 1919 in Yellowstone Park would have knocked his block off if Ned Frost hadn't stopped it with a rifle. And it absorbed five arrows. True, Pope and Young later killed grizzlies without the benefit of a backup rifle, but I suspect that they had an inside track with St. Peter or one of the higherups upstairs.

There are two reasons for having a rifleman handy if you tackle one of the big bears: One, to keep you from getting killed. Two, to keep somebody else from getting killed. There is absolutely no doubt in my

(National Park Service photo)

Grizzly bears present special problems for the bow hunter.

mind that an arrow can do an efficient job on any bear. It has already been proven. However, instead of running away to die as they ought to do, such bears may come running your way to mess up the whole idea. Or, in the event that your arrow isn't properly fitted into the bear, said bear may wander off to take out its mad on somebody else. Unless, of course, you have an expert rifleman at your elbow.

If the guide has to shoot your bear, it is still *your* bear. And, he may not trust your arrow, even though you know it is in the boiler room, and rifle-shoot your bear anyway. So, you have a grizzly, but it isn't a bow kill no matter how well you shot. In fact, at that point it isn't anything but a dead bear unless you want to try to fudge the facts when you get home.

This is not to say that I might not risk such a situation if the opportunity presents itself. But, I would want to spend enough time with my guide to have a perfect understanding so that he wouldn't unnecessarily blow a hole in my hopes.

Also, I think I would like to see him shoot beforehand—at a moving target!

CHAPTER 10

Caribou

Of all the big game beckoning the bow hunter, the majestic caribou is the most available-and-yet-unavailable trophy. This seeming enigma is dictated more by distance than difficulty in downing one of these magnificent creatures. For, once a bow hunter is on the scene, his chances are excellent if conditions are right. On the other hand, hunting caribou with the bow and arrow can be one of the most frustrating and expensive excursions that can be made for any species of big game.

Caribou are found in two general areas, the Arctic fringes of the Northeast and the Northwest. According to A.W.F. Banfield, writing for the National Museum of Canada, there is only one caribou and this includes the reindeer, genus *Rangifer*. However, biologists have generally separated the North American caribou into three species, the barren ground, the mountain, and the woodland caribou. More recently a separate species has been recognized by the Boone and Crockett Club as the Quebec-Labrador caribou. There certainly are differences.

You need only go back to *Outdoor Life's* GALLERY OF NORTH AMERICAN GAME, now a collector's book, published in 1946, to read that woodland caribou heads measure up to "44⅜ inches," as the best

Caribou country!

spread. I have personally seen many caribou in the Ungava Peninsula of northern Quebec where only the woodland caribou was once recognized, which far exceed this spread. However, going for a moment to Boone and Crockett listings, we find that the barren ground caribou of Alaska require a score of 400 to qualify compared to the mountain caribou of 390, the woodland caribou at 295, and the Quebec-Labrador caribou at 375. Pope and Young, at last available information, listed the woodland caribou at 220 score and equated the mountain and the barren ground caribou at 265 each for qualifying scores in bow and arrow competition. This provides at least an insight into what might be considered a trophy head whether taken with the bow or the gun and according to species. The Quebec-Labrador caribou is not listed at this date.

Whether you go to the only state, Alaska, or Alberta, British Columbia, Manitoba, Newfoundland, Quebec, Saskatchewan or the Yukon Territory for caribou, the scenery alone will be worth the trip. For, the caribou is a creature of vast open spaces where only it and a comparatively few other creatures are able to survive the terrible winters which at the same time both threaten and preserve their existence.

Although all other hoofed animals are migratory to some extent, even including the whitetail deer, nomadic habits of the caribou have established it as the wanderer of the Northland. It is this habit of following a seasonal routine that makes it especially vulnerable and an ideal quarry for the bow hunter. Although I have seen gunners take successful shots up to 250 yards, the usual range is 100 yards or less. Sometimes, considerably less.

Despite its comparatively large size, averaging about 300 pounds in the Northeast—considerably more in the now rarer mountain caribou, somewhat less in the barren ground variety—the animal frequently

The range for big bulls is frequently 100 yards or less for the gunner.

is found unprotected by any cover whatsoever. Caribou are the only animals in which the female normally carries a set of antlers. In fact, it is somewhat difficult to distinguish between large cows and young bulls. In one instance, in a slow season during which the usual migration of caribou was absent, a foreign hunter shot a cow which the guide easily convinced him was a bull.

For the bow hunter, or any hunter other than those who take the caribou strictly for food, such as the Indians and Eskimos, antler size becomes the greatest attraction. If a heavy eastern migration is on, when as many as one thousand animals may come through a given area in a matter of a few days, even a bow hunter can afford to be selective. As in any hunting, overeagerness may lead to disappointment if a small bull is taken and then a migration of huge stags comes through after the game tag is filled.

During migrations, caribou tend to be considerably less wary than when they are just idling around in small bunches. Perhaps the reason for this is that the migrations are more or less coincidental with the breeding season, and male animals have other things on their minds.

At least in my experience, it is always a mature cow which leads the herd. Occasionally a small bull may take over, but the final decisions seem to be made by the lead cow. The huge stags, frequently spotted by their nearly white pelage, generally bring up the rear. In fact, they may follow the last of the herd at a considerable distance, mingling only when the bunch stops to reconnoiter or because something has created suspicion or alarm.

In the Northeast, all antlers are usually in velvet at the early part of the season, starting to lose this hide-like coating as cooler weather and the sex urge come on. By the end of the season in late September, most eastern caribou have lost their velvet. Velvet is a consideration in choosing an animal if a choice is indicated by large numbers of caribou, since this antler coating does make the normally large antlers of caribou appear even much larger. Also, it is much more difficult to distinguish individual points when the antlers are in velvet. Although some prefer to retain the antlers with the velvet on if the animal is shot in this condition, most prefer to strip the velvet. This is usually quite easy, particularly as the season develops. Some prefer to soak the antlers in usually available lake or stream water overnight to make the job easier and to avoid a certain amount of blood which frequently runs from the antlers of a freshly-killed caribou.

If you are going bow hunting, the recommendation here is that you go with other archers. As a minimum alternate approach, have a perfect

In September caribou start to shed their velvet as evidenced here.

understanding with your guide about your requirements and stay completely away from those hunting with firearms. Any other approach invites the worst kind of frustration. It is not that gun hunters aren't considerate, it is simply that they do not understand the requirements of the bow hunter.

When an animal is in close proximity, the bow hunter knows that he must normally be perfectly still and take every advantage of terrain and vegetation to increase his chances for a good shot. The gun hunter, particularly in caribou country, becomes so accustomed to seeing the animals at easy ranges and often standing curiously to determine whether or not the hunter poses a hazard to them, that the gunner is apt to be careless in his movements. After all, the animal is usually in open areas where it will be within gun range for a considerable time, even if it does decide to take off.

The ideal range is as close as you can get with the bow. The caribou is a big animal, and it has a fairly heavy growth of hair. You need to have everything possible going for you when you make your try. On a good hit, the caribou will seldom travel much farther than a deer before it goes down. But, since caribou will frequently lie down even if the arrow wound is not an especially good one, the same waiting period of at least a half an hour and possibly more should be employed. If a stalk on a wounded animal is possible because of broken terrain and/or trees and its exact position is known, you may be able to get within sighting range of a downed animal so that you can glass it and make a determination as to the most advisable move.

If you are convinced that the animal is dead, an extremely cautious approach is advisable even before the usual waiting period, and for one important reason. Apparently the powerful digestive acids in a caribou continue working after the animal's death. In a matter of 15 minutes, the stomach can be bloated as though the animal had lain in the heat for a day. According to some Quebec guides, this bloating will spoil the tenderloin for the usual palate. I have been told that Indians prefer the stronger taste which this bloating imparts to the tenderloin and will let the animal lie for at least an hour before eviscerating it.

Some guides will only bring back the front and hind quarters unless you insist on getting more of the meat. There is the tenderloin as well as the filet along the back that constitutes the best part of any animal. It is little short of a crime not to recover it. Consequently, you should insist that this meat be recovered along with the quarters. Of course, you can bring back any part that you wish, and if you are willing to pay the price of transportation, you can bring back every scrap of meat from the animal.

Because airplanes are almost always used in the hunt for caribou to get to and from isolated camps where migrations are expected, there may be some limitations on the amount of meat, the hide, the antlers, and the cape. There is not only the problem of getting it out of camp to a central point, but frequently the trip home will be by airline for at least a part of the distance, and the cost of transporting all this is a financial consideration since the basic cost of the trip is going to be rough no matter where you go.

Although the big migrations provide the best opportunity of taking a caribou with the bow, you cannot always be certain that you will be in the thick of them regardless of the outfitter's past experience. The more conscientious outfitters, such as Fritz Gregor with whom I have hunted in Quebec, will even move you from one camp to another where the hunting is better if necessary.

There are years, too, when the migration will miss the usual camps and it may be necessary to search out small bands of resident caribou. In such instances, you have your work cut out for you. It frequently requires many miles of hunting just to locate caribou. And, since small bands are as previously stated, inclined to be more wary, you must hunt them as you would any other big-game animal. This involves consideration of terrain and air movement as well as the need to get quite close.

As an example of the problems which can be encountered with guides, there was one incident which was actually quite amusing. It involved an Indian guide on one of my hunts. There were plenty of caribou in the area although there was no mass migration at the time, and we had on this occasion walked five or six miles before spotting animals. Two young bulls with fair racks had broken away from their herd and were running across open territory when the Indian spotted them. He insisted that we go galloping up a long rocky hill to intercept them. We did so successfully, but at the spot at which we finally got into position there was but one small bush to use as cover. The Indian practically crawled into the bush, in dog position, and motioned for me to move in close behind him. I did so, and the bush, the Indian, and I presented but one blob on the landscape. I was trying to maneuver an arrow out of my bow quiver as the animals approached to within about 150 yards.

Bloating occurs quickly as evidenced by this animal which a gun hunter abandoned to try for a bigger one. He was apprehended.

Noticing my movement, the Indian said, "No move!"

Meanwhile, I had managed to get an arrow on the string, but the range was too far. I raised the bow behind the Indian's line of vision and waved it back and forth, hoping that it would attract the interest of the two bulls. It did. They gradually moved in until they were about 60 yards away, and I leveled on the larger one. I didn't particularly like the angle of the shot since the animal was quartering toward me. My arrow bounced off his hump. A running shot at the other bull only hurried him on his way as he heard the arrow pass by his rump. The Indian never did know what brought the caribou to within doubtful bow range.

This was not an original move. I had previously discussed this with other hunters who had brought caribou in closer with the same stunt. It is particularly effective when caribou are really into their rut and ready to challenge anything that looks like a threat to their supremacy. At other times, particularly in the early part of the season, any attempt to use their curiosity against them may backfire. You can gain their attention without any trouble. And, they will usually stop to look you over. Just about as often, however, any movement of any kind on your part will start them on their ground-gaining trot for perhaps a mile before they quiet down again.

Relatively heavy hunting in recent years has educated this otherwise usually placid animal. When the guns start talking, the caribou has learned to listen.

Yet, I can recall one day when we tried every device to get rid of a young bull that wanted to accompany my guide and me on our hunt. We waved our arms, shouted to him, even threw rocks in an attempt to discourage him without success. He finally wandered off when we left his territory.

On another occasion, I got up before dawn to post myself at a water hole which was being visited regularly, according to the fresh tracks around it. It turned cold and snowed during the night, and I was anything but comfortable as I waited for action. However, the only caribou that showed was a calf trotting in the distance. About an hour after what would have been sunrise but for the cloud cover, the outfitter and a television cameraman, Harry Allaman, of York, Pennsylvania, left the out-camp to join me. On the way up, Harry had a big caribou stag so close that he couldn't get all the animal in his regular lens, but he obtained some excellent pictures. As long as the camera kept whirring, the caribou stood curious and motionless. As soon as the camera stopped, it took off on a run.

Meanwhile, back at the water hole, the lonely hunter saw abso-

Indian guide builds smudge fire within seconds to attract canoe far down on the lake for our transportation.

lutely nothing more except snowflakes and clouds. When the three of us got together, two cows and their calves moved in to the opposite side of the water hole to provide additional pictures.

On the same trip, a large bull was spotted on a low hill above the alders and the Indian guide and I took off after it, following caribou trails through the thick bushes. It was really a trophy animal. It finally appeared that I had him dead to rights when he stopped behind a white spruce and gave me a chance to move within about 25 yards. However, as I drew back and edged around the tree, I saw another big bull with a somewhat smaller rack that was obviously ready to bolt. The distance was more than twice that of the favored shot, but I cut one loose at him and the arrow bounced off his rear hock. Of course, the big rack went bouncing up through the alders. It was only then that I realized that, in addition to my guide who had been swishing through the brush with oilskins, the outfitter was right behind. Moreover, the cameraman had also come along for the ride, albeit off to one side and out of play! My bull nearly ran him over. Again, Harry's pictures were excellent of the animal that I had mentally, drawn, quartered, and eaten half-way through my first steak.

Wherever you hunt for caribou, you will be in uncertain climate. It pays to go prepared. These animals are found mostly on the high barren hills in the East, but it is usually necessary to slop through swamps bordering the lakes or streams to get to the high ground. Consequently, leak-proof footgear of some kind is in order. My preference is leather because it is the most comfortable for the frequent long walks necessary either to get to migrating animals or to search out resident caribou. Across the Northwest and into Alaska you will also need footgear that can hold up in hunting over the wet terrain frequently encountered there.

When still fresh, before frost turns it gray or it is cropped by caribou, the lichen known as caribou moss is wet and slippery. On one occasion I crawled about one hundred yards on my belly through this stuff trying to approach four big stags before a young bull nearby spooked them all and queered the whole deal. I was soaking wet from contact with the moss despite the fact that we were on a high hill.

You can have sun, rain, sleet and snow, or a combination of all of these in one day when in caribou country, regardless of where it is. Rain gear is a must, and sufficient clothing should be worn so that you can take this weather for extended periods in event you may become lost or weather-bound. It can be mighty uncomfortable wearing extra clothes that may not be needed, but there is no alternative unless you carry a pack-sack to have them in readiness.

No one should venture into caribou country without a compass and a supply of matches in a waterproof container. Even guides can become uncertain of their position. A night in the bush may be preferable to trying to hike back in the dark, particularly if a considerable distance is involved.

It is always well to carry small-game arrows for shots at ptarmigan

Caribou moss, the lichen which is a staple of the caribou, is wet and slippery.

Water is no deterrent to these cows and young bull.

and spruce grouse as well as the occasional snowshoe hare. Although none of these offers much sport with a gun, they can be an interesting break with the bow and arrow. Besides, they provide a welcome change in diet. For the purpose, I usually pack a back quiver so that either the guide or I can carry this extra supply at the ready.

When using a compass in the Northland, you will frequently find that it will be off a considerable number of degrees from True North. This is caused by mineral deposits, and bush pilots must reckon on this error. However, if you use your compass properly by taking bearings when you leave home base, it will still serve its purpose even though it may not agree with the North Star.

Water is no deterrent to caribou, and if it is in their intended path, they simply swim to maintain their direction. This can be a considerable advantage to the bow hunter. You can have your guide drop you off at the edge of the lake or stream and get prepared to shoot when the animal or animals emerge. Or, there are times when the migration is on that the animals just keep coming and you can station yourself in position for a shot where they are making their landing. There is nothing unsporting about this as long as you don't shoot the animals in the water.

There was one occasion when I wanted a guide to land me in front

It is not unusual to find caribou at water's edge.

of a herd of twelve animals containing one good bull. However, there was a gun hunter in the canoe. He shot the animal in the water (after I refused to do so) with a rifle at a distance so close that he was unable to use his telescopic sight. He merely aimed along the barrel of the gun. Fortunately, such gun hunters are in the minority. As it happened, that would have been my one chance on that trip for a bull.

Both resident and migrating caribou will frequently come to water or travel its edges along both lakes and streams. Since the bush usually comes right to the water's edge, it is not unusual to come around a bend

Oil skins and axe are constant companions of guides in caribou country.

to find one or more animals standing within bow range. For this reason, hunting from a canoe is at times preferable to climbing the hills, particularly if animals are on the scarce side. You can cover considerable territory in this manner.

Frequently, if human noise is held to a minimum, a caribou will stand for a bit before melting into the bush. You may get an excellent chance. However, you should practice shooting from whatever position you are limited to in that particular craft. A freighter canoe permits reasonably safe standing, but some of the smaller portage-type craft won't permit you to shift a chew of tobacco without warning the man on the paddle. The larger canoes are usually propelled by an outboard motor, but a good paddler can move you into the shallows silently if game is sighted. Get close. Open expanses of water can foul up your judgment in trying to estimate distance.

Don't go into caribou country without fishing tackle. For, if you score early, there is almost always good fishing somewhere in the area to make the extra days on your trip equally memorable. Of course, you can leave after you make your kill, but the price is usually the same whether you complete your trip or not. So, since for many this is a once-in-a-lifetime journey, go prepared to make the most of it. Lake trout, salmon, char, grayling, brook trout, pike—all or some may be in season.

Hunters await transportation at airport with some excellent caribou racks.

If you do no more than stand upon a hill and breathe deeply of air untainted in an atmosphere that resounds with a great stillness, you will experience a rare treat. There are not many places left in the world where you can be for a time unbothered by insects, airplanes, or anything civilized except your personal pollution. If only to mount the highest promontory in view, come to full draw, and send an arrow into the unknown where but God may mark its falling, it is enough.

But if a majestic set of antlers crests your hill, a pulsating stream of cream-colored movement descends among the distant boulders into your valley, or dark forms split the quiet waters of your lake, you cannot help but tingle with the anticipation that brought you so far.

If your efforts spill blood upon this ground, know that it has ever been so. But, be thankful.

CHAPTER 11

Moose

If you want to go for moose, you have your work cut out for you. This is true whether it is for the awesome monarchs of the Alaskan range, the elusive brutes of the bush in somewhat lower and eastern Canada, or the lordly though a bit smaller moose of western United States.

The moose is big. And, while it is frequently victim of its normal routines and habits, it can hide its great bulk in amazing ways. Talk to any moose hunter who has made a few trips and you will soon be wondering if it is all worth it. It is not unusual to spend a week in areas tracked up like a marshy cow pasture without even seeing or hearing a sign of a moose—and this with a top guide. At this juncture we are talking of the experiences of all hunters!

Not many bow hunters are willing or in the financial position to invest the time and finances to the considerable challenge that moose hunting presents. However, as in all big-game hunting with the bow, you must be sufficiently receptive to the rugged delights and spontaneous vignettes of Nature to count your pleasures equally between what hunting has to offer and what you want to take. Too, you must be willing to accept disappointment, sometimes real hardship, vagaries of weather,

141

and some discomfort. For all of this, the good and the bad, you must pay—rather substantially.

True, there might be the time or times when you can trade most of the previous pessimism for almost instant success. But don't discount any moose kill by a bow hunter just because it came relatively easy. The guy had facing him all the unknown risk factors that exist when he sent his deposit for his moose hunt. Assuming that you don't discourage easily and still want to try for a trophy that doesn't fit the average parlor, let's take a thorough look at what confronts the would-be bow moose hunter.

It must be acknowledged at this point that there are those sufficiently woods-wise and experienced to go it alone with a companion or two; that is, without a guide. The only comment to offer here is simply be damned sure you know what you are doing. Especially the northern bush can be cruel and unforgiving of ineptness.

As an example, an alien gun hunter of my acquaintance went solo 17 days in the Quebec bush without food on an ill-fated moose hunt. He had made his kill and was transporting it by canoe down a rapids where a hidden rock tipped him and his load into the foaming frigid stream. He made it to shore, sans his shoes, but clutching a bit of duffle containing his rifle. A trailing rope on the canoe caught a rock midstream. To measure his chances for survival at that point wouldn't leave much margin for hope. He was many miles from the nearest help.

First he expended his ammunition trying to shoot the rope holding

The moose is big!

the canoe. It was his hope that the craft might then drift to shore. One shot nicked the rope but not enough to free the craft. He finally climbed to a high spot with a piece of tarpaulin for a lean-to and waited for help. It came at last in the form of a helicopter with a rescue party sent to look for him. His feet were frostbitten from snow and cold, and he had lost considerable weight. Otherwise he was okay. But lucky, for a hole in the almost constant fog at his point of rescue was all that made it possible. Had the helicopter missed, he would surely have perished.

The moose is the biggest land animal in North America with size competition coming only from the semi-aquatic Polar bear. Alaskan moose (*Alces gigas*) are largest. However, Canadian bull moose (*Alces americana americana*) average around eight hundred pounds, field dressed. Moose in Wyoming, Montana and Idaho are smallest of the three (*Alces americana shirasi*).

In any case, we are considering a huge animal. The rib arrangement protecting the heart makes a low chest shot difficult to good penetration with any but the most powerful bow. However, the ribs flare sufficiently to permit a good lung shot midway between the back bone and the brisket. A quartering rear shot, forward through the diaphragm, can be effective at almost any spot above the brisket, preferably a bit higher than on a deer.

It is common knowledge that Indians kill moose with the relatively puny .22 caliber rifle. Such shots are frequently taken at the base of the ear. Equally effective with the same bullet is a shot into the neck just short of the jaw cheek. Either, properly placed, will often drop the moose in its tracks.

Consequently, since brush, grass or trees may hide the more desirable chest area, a neck shot well toward the head should be effective with an arrow. It should only be considered at close range. But, in considering tackle, take into account that a moose's hide alone is up to a quarter of an inch thick. Its winter hair coat is extremely dense and heavy. Even the meat between the heavy ribs is about two inches thick on a big moose.

If you are going on a private hunt, care of the meat can be a major consideration. Best hunting with the bow comes in the rutting season. The weather will usually be frosty, but it can turn warm. Commercial hunts are usually fly-in tent camps. But, if sloppy weather socks in and the temperature turns warm after a kill, the plane may not be able to respond to a radio call or make a fly-over to check your camp. Cheesecloth to cover the quartered carcass is a must in any event just to keep insects and dirt away from the meat.

Commercial hunts are usually fly-in tent camps.

Unless you have seen the quartered carcass of a moose, it is difficult to visualize the transportation problem that even a small moose presents. Bulk and weight of an average moose will be roughly eight times the equivalent of an average deer, whether field-dressed or skinned down to the bare carcass. If you take a bull with sizable antlers and you want to mount your trophy, just getting this part of the animal —head, antlers, cape—out of the bush is a major transportation challenge.

Don't consider anything less than a station wagon for over-the-road transport if you plan to bring a moose home. And, no more than two hunters should plan to ride together. You will be bringing out everything you take in with the exception of food. With luck, you will barely have room for even one moose and your duffle. Of course, if you have a trailer, truck, or other more spacious accommodation, plan accordingly. Load limit of your vehicle is also a consideration.

Is the preceding an attempt to discourage bow hunting for moose? Definitely not! However, it most certainly is intended as a caution to anyone contemplating such a trip.

Okay. You still want to go?

Try to get in as early as possible. Your best chance with the bow is during the rut when moose are moving and will respond to a call. The weather can foul you up if it stays warm and delays the sex urge. Since you must usually make plans and reservations many months ahead, you have no control over this eventuality and must take your chances.

One thing is certain. Moose movement, or lack of it, will be governed by the weather.

If you are early, moose will still be hanging around the swamps and lakes. During the rut it will be much the same with the added advantage that you can have the moose hunting you—that is, providing you will be calling them. For a period of a week or so after the rut, moose will just be standing around in the bush. It is probably the most difficult period to hunt either with bow or gun. Following this the animals will be found in areas of good browse as they return to active feeding, frequently on cut-over ridges or old burns. During periods of really dirty weather they will seek the heaviest swamp area thickets.

It is impossible to make a recommendation as to whether the individual should hunt by land or by water. It will depend upon both the time and the place. However, in either method, a boat or a canoe may be employed.

A canoe, with a good man on the paddle, is best if everything else is in order. For example, on one personal trip it was necessary to utilize an extremely tippy canoe. It was only 12 inches deep from gunwale to bottom of the craft. This made it impractical to shoot my 60-inch bow

Wawa, Ontario, is the hub for good moose hunting in all directions.

A good canoe handler can move you silently along.

in the accustomed vertical position. With practice, from a sitting position, I could cant the bow and still shoot reasonably well. However, except from a ninety degree angle, it was impossible to attain full draw. Only 16 feet long and 33 inches wide, the canoe was much too unsteady to permit a standing shot although the Indian guide was superb on the paddle.

An archer needs everything going for him. Either the canoe or the boat should be stable enough to permit standing or the seat should be sufficiently high to provide lower limb clearance for the bow.

When moose are frequenting lakes and marshes, a good canoe

If you get an opportunity, shoot! The moose won't wait.

handler can move you along silently. By hugging shore, you have a chance for a shot at a moose standing just inside the bush or in a marsh. It will usually stand briefly, long enough for careful aim, but don't wait. The animal's limited vision and inherent curiosity may still not permit delay.

Whether going by water to a calling spot or just hunting in this manner, your chances are good for action. Talk should be held to an absolute minimum at the level of a whisper or be eliminated entirely. Sound travels fantastically well over water.

If calling is to be employed and the route of the moose can be anticipated, the archer should be stationed in a position to intercept the animal. This may require that the caller be sitting in the canoe some distance from the bow hunter. Or, both may be in the same cover. But, and this is so important, the caller must be impressed with the need to stay hidden and immobile.

Good callers seldom call often. Ten minutes, usually much longer, is the minimum span of time between calls. Calls are rarely made when a bull approaches. He knows the general direction, usually the exact spot, from which the cow call has emanated. If he is hesitant, a soft bull grunt may bring him on the double. He suspects competition for the imaginary cow's favors.

Too much calling can queer the whole deal. If a bull responds back in the bush, but won't come out, he probably has a cow with him or he is suspicious. If a cow is nearby and she has already been serviced, a bull call, or grunt, may even send her away. A young bull may hold back because he is afraid to mix it up with what may sound like a big bruiser to him. As in hunting wild turkeys, many are called, but few are fooled.

If the rut is over, or nearly so, it may be necessary to hit the bush. Although wind is a great deterrent to success during the rutting season, it can work to your advantage when scouting the bush. It is possible to move up on a sleeping animal. Or, you may get sufficiently close that the moose might jump up and make the customary inspection of its intruder before freight-training its way through seemingly impenetrable bush.

Of course you must work upwind. It may be necessary to walk miles to get into position for such hunting. But, here again, water transportation can be a tremendous advantage.

Many moose are called, but few are fooled.

Keep watching your back track. It is easy to bypass a moose in heavy cover. The animal may allow you to walk by before arising to determine what you are and what you are up to. If with a guide, allow him a reasonable distance ahead of you for this reason. The moose may pop out of its bed close by. Or, the guide may spot a resting animal and motion you forward for the shot.

Since few guides have had bow hunters on a moose try, you should have had long and detailed discussions with yours about your requirements. In the period just following the mating urge, moose are tough to come by, even with the gun. Experienced guides know when this period occurs just by the type of food or browse the animals seek.

I once asked an Indian guide if, "the bull goes off his feed during the rut?"

He answered, "Only in the front."

After mulling this around in my mind a bit, I decided it didn't quite fit the question.

"What do you mean?"

"Only the front foots come off the ground," he explained.

Enjoying a private laugh, I let it go at that. Obviously he had thought I said *feet*.

Although a guide is probably best versed in such matters, there is the matter of what biologists and scientists properly call scats, or droppings. These are to moose the same as buffalo chips are to buffaloes. In the vernacular of the bush they have a more common, plainer name.

When trying to interpret the tracks of moose, these take on special significance, particularly if the animals are difficult to find. In the first place, the adult moose, according to word in the best bush circles, can be identified by the results of their last good meal. A bull drops round waste in a heavy mound similar to, but smaller in size than that of a horse and it is more compact. An adult female leaves a bit smaller, slightly elongated pellets. Nearby is frequently the much smaller and round pellets of the calf. All are black when fresh.

If the excrement is steaming, it may be from moments to a half-hour old. If still wet and shiny, it is likely from the night before or has been deposited within hours. If still black and firm, but minus its wet sheen, it is probably of the day before. Once a tinge of brown can be seen as drying takes place, the evidence might be from days to weeks old and has little relevance to your hunt.

Tracks provide certain information if you can find good prints. If you discover muddy water in a print, look around carefully. You may be in immediate business. If filled with clear water and the print has sharp edges in mud, or if grass or moss is still impressed flat in the track, a moose probably passed within hours or the night before. In snow, the type of snow, outside temperature and depth of print give their own information. But, such prints are actually tough to interpret, depending upon the weather.

The important point behind all this is the necessity to get close to your game. You want to know whether the animal is spending time in the area or is just passing through. Anything important to the gun hunter may be doubly important to the archer.

Whether to take a cow, or even a calf, depends a lot on what the kill means to you. I once passed up a chance in Quebec at what both the guide and I thought was a cow, and we called in a gun hunter who shot the animal. It turned out to be a young bull with little more than branching spikes which were not visible until it turned its head toward the gunner. That was before I learned how tough it is to get a bow shot at a moose—any moose.

Many cows, even calves, are shot by gun hunters. Those after meat prefer a cow or a calf. Indians will usually take a cow or a young bull, if possible, for winter meat.

How dangerous is a moose?

Well, like bear stories, there are countless tales of moose attacks. Most are from imagination and by cows in the calving season and can be discounted for the hunting experience. I have interviewed—not just talked to—a great many guides and outfitters. None knew of anyone being hurt by a moose when hunting.

Edward Sayers, Ojibway Indian and one of the finest guides I have ever had the pleasure of hunting with, had two experiences with mean moose in 25 years of guiding and hunting for himself in Ontario. His hunting has been in the excellent territory around the Wawa area where he was born.

The one attack, he admitted, was mostly open to conjecture. He had cornered a bull in a box of big rocks, and there was only one way out—where Ed stood. The bull tried to take it, but Ed dropped him as he was coming head-on.

Considerably more serious was the second instance in which Sayers was hunting with a buddy for winter meat. They came onto two bulls and two cows with calves in a fairly open meadow dotted with small black spruce. Ed's first shot dropped one of the cows and the other moose scattered. Just before the cow died, she let out a distressed bawl.

Out of the bush came charging the bigger bull, one with a spread

Ed Sayers, Ojibwa Indian, proved to be an excellent guide and camp man.

of 59 inches. It came straight for Ed! He didn't want to shoot, but he felt he was forced to when the animal was coming head down only about 15 yards away. Ed's .32 Special dropped the bull in a heap, but it bounced straight back up. He managed to hit it again before ducking to one side as his buddy opened up. When the bull was finally down for keeps, it had taken a total of seven hits!

Even smart gun hunters will wait out a moose that is hit but does not drop to the shot. If possible, at least an hour should elapse before taking the trail. When an animal seems to be traveling well, a second wait is in order, even on the trail. No one likes to leave a carcass out overnight, but this is preferable to losing the animal by pressing it too soon or too hard.

A bow-shot animal will generally be well bled out whenever it is found—even though the bleeding is internal. If the nights are cool, usually the case, there should be no problem with the meat. In any event, every possible effort should be expended to recover so magnificent a creature.

Sometimes there is fear that wolves will eat at a carcass. It may be possible, but unlikely. Even if this should occur, the amount of meat that these animals might get is a lesser loss much preferable to losing the entire animal. I have never known of wolves bothering a field-dressed animal of any kind. Once human scent is on it, wolves stay away.

So, you still want to take a moose with the bow? More power to you. Certainly you will be one of a small group of archers who really take their bow hunting seriously. You are in for some interesting times, no matter when or where you hunt.

However, as when hunting for any of the really large game species with the bow, you carry a heavy weight of responsibility when you release an arrow. True, this is another member of the deer family. But a moose is not as easily replaced as the more common and prolific white-tails and the mule deer that have fewer natural enemies and hardships to endure in the better range. If you are a serious bow hunter, you know the deadliness of a sharp broadhead. But, when you release it at so magnificent a quarry as a moose, you should have everything going for you to anticipate a clean kill. An animal that may weigh from eight hundred to eighteen hundred pounds on the hoof is an awesome challenge.

Unless you really know the territory, you should *have a guide.*

It takes guts, it takes skill, it takes stamina, it takes cash—to hunt for moose with the bow and the arrow. But, even more important, it takes all that the word *sportsman* connotes.

Except for moose in the contiguous states, it means going to Alaska or one of the Canadian provinces for statesiders—Alberta, British Columbia, Manitoba, Newfoundland, Ontario, Quebec, Saskatchewan, Yukon Territory. Unless you are a resident, you may be required to have a guide. (See appendix) In fact, unless you are a resident or you are quite familiar with the territory, you *should* have a guide.

Since there are no special provisions for archers, you will be hunting against the guns. This is no serious problem in the more remote areas. You will likely be the only hunter for miles around. You may be tempted to take a gun as an alternate arm. If so, forget the bow. The temptation to substitute the more reliable arm will probably be overpowering.

Whether to have a backup gun carried by the guide or another hunter is your choice. If so, be sure you have an understanding that you will call the shots. Rather than have a badly hit animal escape, that you feel may not be recovered, you may want this edge. Of course, any assistance immediately discounts the trophy as a bow kill.

There is no intent here to discourage anyone from hunting moose with the bow. Rather, the desire is to encourage both mental and physical conditioning for this great archery endeavor. You need only study the records of Pope and Young Club to know that it can be and it has been done with impressive results.

There are few greater thrills in bow hunting.

CHAPTER 12

Antelope

Coming slowly over a rise along the nearly dry bed of the Cheyenne River in Wyoming, where a herd of about thirty pronghorns had been hanging out, it was the driver's hope to spot these animals from a distance. Then we could alight and make a stalk for them. However, he overshot a bit, and the jeep was suddenly exposed to the entire herd.

We made a scramble and tried to head them off enough to be in shooting position. But trying to head off an antelope is akin to trying to head off a shooting star. Anyway, it was a glorious sight to watch these beautiful creatures stampede in a line that ebbed and flowed up across the prairie to a high hill. I put my binocular on them and watched until they assembled in a spread-out group to contemplate the next move. They had run full tilt up the hill for—including a pass in front of us requiring a wide sweep—a total distance of perhaps three-quarters of a mile. Yet, as I watched, the lead buck of the herd serviced a doe. In fact, he did it again. One needs only to see one antelope to find many reasons to admire them. This fellow had tossed in an additional reason that any red-blooded, healthy male can appreciate.

But, after seeing an antelope in action when it has been alarmed or is running just for the hell of it, it makes one wonder how anyone could take one with the bow and arrow. Yet, Montana reported a 16 percent success ratio for bow hunters in 1970 out of 214 who were licensed.

Although there are fourteen states which have antelope hunting, there are actually only six which offer hunting to nonresidents. Top pronghorn producers are the states of Wyoming, Montana and New Mexico. If you know your way around or have resident connections, some fairly good hunting is also available to nonresidents in Arizona, Colorado and Idaho. In the best states, licenses are obtainable in most areas through a drawing system which requires an early application.

As with other types of hunting far afield, a trip for an Easterner into antelope states is a pleasurable experience in any event. However, taking an antelope with a bow and arrow is a special feat and certainly is the high point of any such excursion.

Before we go looking for this not-so-elusive but hard-to-hunt animal, let's take a little preview of what it is. Unlike the elk, the moose, and the buffalo, which were pushed out of their native habitat in the East, the antelope is strictly a Westerner. In fact, its primary food is sagebrush. However, it will subsist on succulent plants which serve as a source of both food and water in very barren regions.

The antelope is one of a kind. In fact, *Antilocapra americana* is in no way related to the European antelope and some feel it is best identi-

The pronghorn antelope is one of a kind.

fied as a *pronghorn*, taken from the distinctive head adornment worn by the males.

The sheath of these horns is shed annually in the manner of antlers except that the bony cores remain permanently. The main horns are erect and branch into two prongs, with the longer extending backward and inward. The record head had 20-inch horns. Anything over ten is quite respectable.

Although hunters are accustomed to working hard just to get sight of their quarry, not so with the pronghorn. If you are in antelope country, it is quite common to see anywhere from one to a great many of these animals curiously watching you from a distance. They are not hard to spot. The reddish-brown overcoat with white underparts, white flanks and cheeks, and two distinctive white bands at the throat make it easy to locate and identify. Going away, it has a white rump patch somewhat of the same appearance as the whitetail deer's flag. Most animals depend upon protective coloration to a large extent in evading their enemies. The pronghorn depends upon its excellent vision and fleetness of foot.

It is true that the antelope is curious. It was once fairly easy to lure them within rifle range by waving a white handkerchief or something similar to take advantage of their inquisitiveness. This is much tougher today, particularly after the first shot is fired in gunning season. Bow hunters may have a better chance, but any movement is as apt to send

The pronghorn depends upon its excellent vision and fleetness of foot.

the animals out of the county as to bring them within bow range. But their curiosity can still be used against them in some instances.

One morning when my son, Keith, was building a deer blind of sage in Wyoming, a buck antelope came up to inspect the job. In fact, it hung around within a 60-yard range for quite some time. Unfortunately, my son had neglected to take his bow along.

At another time, he made a stalk which would seem to disprove the stories about the animal's telescopic vision. He had moved in up-wind on a herd of seven does and two bucks, but the range was still too far for shooting. Taking inches at a time, it took him about an hour to cover 100 yards and bring him within about 45 yards' range of the pronghorns. Although he normally can bunch his arrows in a nine-inch circle at that distance, he emptied his bow quiver before sending the antelope down to me. (He is a former Pennsylvania barebow champion.) I waited out the herd, passing single file at about 50 yards, when the buck bringing up the rear stopped. I had a lousy release and sent my arrow into a tree. The buck obligingly loped past another of our group who proceeded to miss it at 12 yards.

The preceding is not to advertise our poor shooting so much as to illustrate that antelope can be taken with the bow and arrow. In fact, one of our group did score the next day in the same patch of cotton-woods.

This also illustrates one way in which to get shooting. Cottonwood and quaking aspen frequently grow along streams where the general terrain is bare of cover. In the bow hunting seasons which precede the gunning seasons, the weather is usually still quite warm. Antelope will seek out the shade of trees which provide solitary ropes of green that tie together the prairies and foothills where the pronghorn is frequently found.

The best bow hunting frequently comes during the antelope's rutting season. They are herd animals and the largest and most vigorous bucks will accumulate a gathering of does for their own satisfaction. Younger bucks, which have been unable to attract does to them, will work the fringe areas of a herd in hopes of attracting an unfaithful female. These attempts are frequently greeted by a charge from the lead buck, and the younger male will take to his heels. In these sweeps to and from the fringes of a herd, the younger males frequently expose themselves to a hidden bow hunter.

This is also true to some degree wherever the animals are found. It is not at all unusual to see a solitary buck more or less aimlessly wandering around and probably cussing out his luck. He has been driven from a herd or has given up in discouragement and is looking for a harem of his own. At such times these wanderers seem more curious, likely because they are seeking company. A stalk on such animals has a chance of being productive. Or it may be possible to get ahead of it for a pass shot.

Never underrate the visual acuity of the pronghorn. You must be completely hidden as you move into position. Unlike stalking deer when you can hide behind a tree only half the width of your outline, or where it is possible to gain ground with considerable personal exposure if the deer's attention is diverted to browsing or grazing, the pronghorn never seems to be unaware of *any* movement. Yet, it is not infallible. As in my son's situation, previously mentioned, if movements are slow enough, they *may* escape detection.

And, again that inherent curiosity of the animal may give you a break. If only a small part of you shows, the pronghorn may actually come toward you to investigate. This is particularly true if your approach is at an oblique angle rather than a frontal one. But, don't count on it!

Of course, the desire is always to go for that lead buck since he is more likely to have a trophy set of horns. Where it is known that antelope travel through, tree stands can be effective in getting shots at the larger bucks.

The water hole where the antelope herd faked us out.

Drives can also be set up in wooded areas when a number of hunters are working together. Of course, the tendency of the antelope to run for long distances before even considering a rest stop must be taken into consideration. If really alarmed, the lead buck will take his herd completely out of the trees onto open ground, and the hunting effort is lost. If not pushed too hard, the herd may run for a distance in the stand of trees and then stop to reconnoiter.

If water holes are known, these make excellent spots at which to set up a blind to wait for an antelope. This can be particularly effective if the season has been especially dry. The animals normally will come to water sometime after daylight is well on its way. They will usually be found in such areas up to about 10 o'clock in the morning before they move out to other parts.

The tendency of the antelope to run, seemingly just for the pure joy of it, can work both for and against the bow hunter. It can be most discouraging to make a long stalk through trees, or sage or gullies only to have the animal decide to take off for no apparent reason. At other times, it is just as apt to run into a hunter while on one of these cross-country marathons. Consequently, it is important to keep alert at all times.

This is why a guide who knows the area can be particularly useful. On a hunt at the ranch of Jim Zerbst in eastern Wyoming, he took me to a canyon where there was a water hole which is frequented by his horses. We approached cautiously from the top side. There were no pronghorns at the watering hole, but a small band had apparently just departed. They were down the canyon a bit and caught us flatfooted as we peered over the edge. In seconds they were up the far side to provide some long shooting in a strong wind when two bucks stood for a time to plan their next move with the small herd of does.

When archery seasons are in, most areas permit the hunter to take any pronghorn. However, the determination of most archers is to take an adult male for a wall trophy. This desire sometimes fades toward the tail end of the hunt after it is discovered how tough it is to get an antelope, *any* antelope.

Camouflage clothing is most essential when hunting for antelope. And, since the animals depend to a great degree upon their excellent eyesight as a means of protection, all movement should be calculated beforehand. Stay away from tops of ridges and hills. An antelope can spot you many hundreds of yards away under normal conditions, but if you are exposed on the horizon, any antelope within a mile or more is likely to spot your movements.

One peculiarity of the pronghorn which can be used against it is its reluctance to jump any great hurdle. In some areas of the West where sheep fences are common, the antelope has learned to take them when necessary. However, I have seen an entire herd search desperately for an opening in such a fence when it was no more than five feet high. The herd ran frantically back and forth after a few of the lead animals had gotten through beneath the fence until the entire number had made it to the other side. There they bunched up and took off on a run.

Since these spots are frequently known to the animals, an archer can station himself in a blind nearby and have a good chance to get shooting. If the wind is right, antelope can actually be driven toward such areas although it can never be anticipated for certain what direction they will take. If possible, they will avoid the fence entirely or make a wide sweep to get around whoever or whatever has disturbed them. In areas where herds are fairly well defined and there is some pattern to their movements, these pass-through areas can make excellent hunting stations.

But because the antelope is a creature of the wide open spaces, prediction of their movements is usually a guess at best. Probably the safest prediction is that they will avoid fences in any way possible. In some areas of the West the mortality is extremely high where fences are prevalent since the animals frequently get tangled up in these artificial barriers.

When it comes to archery tackle for antelope, whatever works well for deer is right for this quarry. Since aluminum arrows are the fastest among materials currently available, they would seem to be the best choice for the antelope. The arrow isn't going to outrun this fleet creature, but shots are inclined to be farther than the average deer shot. And pronghorns are somewhat smaller than the average deer, standing up to about three feet high at the shoulders and averaging somewhere between ninety and one hundred pounds.

They are tough animals, nevertheless, so you need plenty of bow behind that arrow. The preferred target area is somewhat smaller than on the average deer, but a chest shot should provide a clean kill. The antelope's speed may take it farther than the average deer that is mortally wounded. But, there is a fair chance that you will be able to mark the animal down by sight on the kind of terrain which they usually inhabit.

Although the does carry somewhat rudimentary horns, bucks are easily distinguished by their much larger horns and black face, particularly on the older and more desirable specimens.

Black face and much larger horns usually identify the more desirable males.

Since bow hunting for antelope frequently comes during days when the weather may be quite warm, special thought should be given beforehand to preservation of the meat. This is particularly true if your hunt is to be far away from the nearest community boasting a walk-in cooler. If it is necessary to hang the carcass in camp, some provision for shading the meat as well as covering it to guard against insects and dirt should certainly be made.

The common way for gun hunters to go after antelope, where possible, is to ride in an off-the-road vehicle or truck until the animals are sighted. Then everybody scrambles to the ground and starts shooting. Although such vehicles are handy for the bow hunter, no amount of this kind of chasing is likely to produce shooting with the bow and arrow. The archer must be prepared to do plenty of walking no matter how close he may be able to approach to pronghorns with a vehicle or how far he gets ahead of a herd.

The love of running, previously mentioned, sometimes produces an impromptu race between antelope and vehicle. The animals will often pace a vehicle for some distance. Then they will almost invariably cut across the path of the vehicle as though to demonstrate their scorn for the man-made conveyances. Except on the very best of roads, the antelope always wins.

Camouflage is important, but footwear can be just as important. Days are hot and nights are from cool to cold in most pronghorn habitat. Don't dress too heavy for the chill of the morning if you expect to be gone for the day. It can get hot.

There is some danger from snakes although reasonable care will eliminate the possibility of being struck by a rattler. Since you will sometimes be climbing over rough terrain, be careful stepping over rocks or reaching for support where a snake may be disturbed into striking. Whether you want to wear high shoes or boots is a personal

choice. Certainly they are a safeguard against snake bite. However, such footgear can be most cumbersome and warm during the middle of the day. An extra pair of heavy trousers under a camouflage suit and high stockings will provide some margin of protection although it certainly won't prevent fangs from finding flesh. But it can minimize the effects of a snake bite.

At one time there was an estimated forty million antelope on the western plains. Market hunting, which brought the price down to one dollar for a whole carcass, greatly depleted the herds until fear was held for their preservation. Strict law enforcement followed and the antelope has made an excellent comeback.

The doe normally drops two fawns and occasionally triplets. It is now estimated that there are between one-quarter of a million and three hundred thousand antelopes in fifteen western states and southwestern Canada. It is third only to the whitetail and mule deer in numbers.

There is something special about having a mounted antelope head as a trophy. Although barring disease, there is practically no chance of it becoming extinct, it is one of a kind among all the animals of the world. It has no counterpart either on this or other continents. Gun hunters, too, consider it a real prize.

Consequently, to an archer the pronghorn will forever be one of the most rewarding trophies of all.

CHAPTER 13

The High Heads–
Sheep and Goats

My first introduction to a Rocky Mountain ram was something less than impressive. It was in the Canadian province of Alberta, north of Banff at spring run-off, although we were over a week into the summer. The ram was shedding and his coat was a mess. However, the massive sweep of his three-quarter curl was a reminder of what this elegant animal would look like later when he moved back into the higher elevations.

Shortly after, some equally scrubby Rocky Mountain goats posed briefly on a crag before picking their way up a precipitous slope. But, these were shaggy park specimens and a far cry from the neatly rumpled winter coat of these animals when and where hunting for them is permitted. For, with the exception of the desert bighorn, sheep and goats of western area states and Canada are creatures of the high country where animals less endowed to combat the wind and cold would surely perish.

From the journalistic standpoint it might seem cowardly to lump all sheep and goats into one chapter. However, you need only go to the listings of Pope and Young records to discover that trying to cover individual hunting for each of these mutton makers could alone fill this book to say nothing of trying to also cover the native American goat.

163

Rocky Mountain sheep.

Pope and Young records, in addition to the Rocky Mountain goat (which is not a goat at all but is considered to be a type of antelope) recognize not less than four members of the sheep family: the stone sheep, white or Dall sheep, big-horned sheep, and desert sheep.

Resident hunters of states and provinces which have sheep and/or goat hunting are quite aware of requirements set up to hunt for any of these species. Others had best set their sights somewhere from Arizona (or even down into Mexico) up through western mountain ranges, particularly the Rockies, through the Canadian provinces of Alberta, British Columbia, and the Yukon Territory and on into Alaska. A check of the appendix will give the states and provinces that provide this type of hunting for the archer.

An excellent rundown on the various species of sheep and the Rocky Mountain goat is contained in the latest edition of THE HUNTER'S ENCYCLOPEDIA (Stackpole Books).

For our purposes, we are chiefly concerned with what to expect on the hunt for these animals as well as physical requirements and archery tackle. Except for the desert sheep, you will be hunting high, or higher. Although some of the animals will winter on the lower slopes, they are generally found well above timberline. This is particularly true of the goat.

Although sheep were at one time well distributed over the western states, market hunters took their toll. Even more destructive were diseases carried by imported domestic sheep. Take-over of the better grass lands also diminished the wild flocks substantially. Although they are being maintained through careful conservation practices, there is no possibility that they will ever return in great numbers because of domestic competition on available range. Regulated hunting actually seems to have little or no effect on the total populations and is probably healthy for them in the long run.

Because hunting either sheep or goats is today a most demanding exercise, a guide is practically a must either because of law or by choice. In any case, the hunter has his work cut out for him in big, jagged chunks of rocky mountain, pulverized slate slopes, snow fields, and precipitous dropoffs.

From the smallest to the largest of the collective animals, in the case of sheep we are considering a chunky animal of from about 200 to 350 pounds. Since only the method of hunting sheep and goats varies from other hunting to some degree, archery tackle for each conforms somewhat to that used for deer. But, those who can handle heavier tackle well are advised to carry it. Any animal that can take the rugged terrain in which sheep and goats are found is certain to have plenty of stamina. Also, the possibility of loss is great in the broken country they inhabit when plenty of power is not behind the arrow.

Except for the desert variety, and even they are frequently found in the toughest type of arid terrain, sheep like steep, rocky hideaways. The sheep hunter must be physically able to handle high altitudes and be mentally able to take the sometimes dizzy heights to which it is necessary to climb. Of course, there are happy occasions when animals can be found where they can be approached on horseback, but more often the hunter has to have a bit of mutton in his own constitution to approach close enough for good shooting.

For the preceding reasons, a pair of shoes that will provide firm footing where there is none, and clothes which will withstand cool to cold temperatures after a good sweat is worked up, are essential.

Whether hunting sheep or goats, and whether in the broken terrain of desert country or the high elevations between the trees and the snow, it is necessary to get above the animals to improve chances for success.

Instinctively these creatures know that their troubles come from below, and they will seek the heights to escape any suspected danger.

Rock nests, built possibly centuries ago by Indians, have been found at some of the higher elevations by mountain climbers who thought they were first to ascend the heights. John Muir, founder of the Sierra Club, was among the first to report that the Paiute Indians hunted sheep in the High Sierras where discoveries of heads and horns and obsidian arrowheads provided evidence of this activity. Other reports have shown sheep tracks at over the 14,000-foot level. This certainly does not mean that it is necessary to go to these elevations to find sheep, but it does mean that a hunter must be prepared to hit the high elevations on occasion for any chance of success. Of course, just how high it is necessary to go is somewhat determined by the weather encountered during the season.

In any event, preparation should be made to survive in some of the roughest and most spectacular country on the North American continent.

Hunting will be determined by the seasons permitted, but the rut carries its own significance. A guide, whether you slip down into Mexico or head for the high places in the Rocky Mountain chain, or

Hit the high country for sheep and goats.

farther north, is certainly recommended, if not mandatory. You should have enough interchange of correspondence before attempting such a hunting trip to know, within reason, just what to expect.

In the high country, you will need a binocular considerably more powerful than what may be fine for other game. A good part of your time may be spent just scanning the terrain for sign of a sheep. For, except during migration periods, most hunting is for specific animals that are first spotted and then stalked to their beds.

Although sheep are not noted for their powers of scent, and their hearing is adjusted to the occasional miniature slides of shale or stone, their eyesight is phenomenal. Since most accounts in the outdoor magazines involve gun hunters shooting flat-trajectory bullets over long ranges, there may be the feeling that a bow hunter simply doesn't have a chance. This certainly is not true since many gun shots are taken at fairly close ranges, within 35 or 40 yards. Even closer shots are possible. It is all a matter of chance and stalking ability. But, since the stamina required to live in such places is obviously great, these animals are tough, and every effort should be made to get into as positive a shooting situation as possible. And, the usual waiting period after a hit is advisable. Otherwise a weakened animal might go plunging into a crevasse, or over a cliff to an inaccessible recovery spot, or smash its horns in a sickening death drop.

Less desirable as a trophy and far down on the preferred list of big game for eating, the Rocky Mountain goat is nevertheless sufficient challenge to bring out the best in a bow hunter.

This is somewhat immaterial to the bow hunter who knows that he must hit the high spots for this shaggy white aerialist that may weigh anywhere from 150 to 300 pounds on the hoof. Both males and females have horns, and it is next to impossible for the average hunter to distinguish between the two when side by side and with no kids around. Both are white the year around with an occasional brown marking on the mane and tail. The short, sharp black horns are not overly impressive, and will average somewhere around nine inches in length.

Unlike the sheep, the Rocky Mountain goat's vision is considered only fair, and its hearing doesn't distinguish it. However, its sense of smell is quite acute and must be always considered in hunting. During the hunting season, older goats are usually alone and the nannies will be traveling with their kids and the younger males.

Although it also usually means plenty of climbing, by comparison with sheep hunting the taking of a goat is not considered nearly so difficult. Experienced hunters, after marking an animal with the binocu-

(Montana Fish and Game photo by Craig Sharpe)

A Rocky Mountain goat can bring out the best in a bow hunter.

lar, will usually wait out a feeding billy to give him a chance to fill up and find a place for a nap. Success of a stalk is usually greatly improved after the goat beds down for the day. It is then less apt to wander off and be absent at the end of a difficult stalk.

Although it is always desirable to get as impressive a head as possible, the bow hunter should be well satisfied with any Rocky Mountain goat. Whether or not it is difficult, or relatively easy, finding and taking this creature in its normal habitat is a bow hunting accomplishment that rates high on the list.

In a somewhat lesser vein, but still high on the list of achievements for bow hunters, is the hunting of feral sheep and goats. Among the spots popular with bow hunters is Santa Catalina Island off the California coast. It is privately owned, but hunting for feral goats is permitted. Farther up the coast among the Channel Islands is Santa Cruz where a herd of sheep exists which draws archers from a large area.

Even farther west, the best feral sheep and goat hunting can be found on the Hawaiian Islands, particularly on the big island of Hawaii itself. Of all the places I have ever hunted, the Island of Hawaii provides some of the worst terrain that is possible to imagine. But it is in such areas of volcanic jumble that some of the better hunting is found.

Both sheep and goats have been on the island for nearly two hundred years or so, and in that time they have learned to subsist on the sparse vegetation and morning dew as the only water available in many areas. Best hunting is in between two of the record mountain masses in the world, Mauna Loa, largest; and Mauna Kea, highest (from the

Joe Moke took the first hitch packing my ram out through the Hawaiian lava and pili grass.

ocean floor). The saddle created by these peaks is shared by a military reservation, and it contains some of the most unusual hunting to be found anywhere in the world. A reasonable challenge to gunners, the area is a real bonanza for bow hunters who should have a little bit of sheep and goat blood in them for a starter. The combination of wariness developed by these one-time domestic animals coupled with the horrendous terrain is an experience to compare with some of the more difficult hunts encountered anywhere.

My first hunt was with Joe Moke, native Hawaiian, who took me for sheep along the base of Mauna Kea over rotted old volcanic ash, known as aa, which is covered with pili grass to hide the many jagged edges and holes that are real ankle busters. We jumped a number of vari-colored animals before I made a successful shot on a small black ram. Enroute we passed up one of the Polynesian pigs that have run wild for some one thousand or so years. Fortunately, too, for back-packing the ram over the lava was chore enough for one day. We finally saw some full-curl rams that were temporarily protected since it was an off-day for shooting on the military reservation where we spotted them.

Later, Jimmy Lee, Chinese-American who runs the archery shop in the main city of Hilo, led me over some of the newer lava on a goat hunt. We finally made a successful stalk on a herd that numbered some seventy animals. Jimmy insisted on carrying the two beheaded carcasses a half-mile or so over lava that looked like the careless offal of a giant coke oven. Although the goats could run over this stuff at full tilt, each that was taken had the characteristic callouses on their knees from contact with the rough lava that not even they could avoid.

Any bow hunter going to the Hawaiian Islands would do well to pack a take-down in his suitcase. A nonresident license is only $15.00, bow or gun. The trip up into the interior is a long-to-be-remembered experience.

Sheep or goats, whether native and wild or feral and wild, are among the most interesting quarry to be sought with the bow and arrow. It is seldom that any of them comes easy. But the lure and the lair of all sheep and goats will ever have special meaning to an archer who lifts his eyes to the high places.

CHAPTER 14

Elk

The second largest member of the deer family, the elk, is known more properly as the wapiti. Its less publicized name stems from Indian sources which allude to its white rump and tail. The name is akin to the Cree *wapitew*, meaning white or whitish, but comes directly from the Shawnee *wapiti*. Although similar to the European deer, the American elk is considerably larger and is one of the top trophies of North America for both gun and bow hunters.

Because of its size, elk hunting demands from the bow hunter the best tackle available and much of the know-how needed for moose hunting. However, whereas the moose is a creature of swamps and low wooded hills, the lordly elk is monarch of the high places for the most part. This, at least, until his eminence descends with the seasons to reign in dignity until Nature annually robs him of the great rack of antlers that sets him apart from others of the deer family. He is finally reduced to a station little higher than the harem of cows that he worked so hard to collect the season before.

Almost every account of elk hunting starts out with a climb to the high country by horse or vehicle, depending somewhat upon the season.

(Utah State Division of Wildlife Resources photo)

The Wapiti is one of the top trophies for both gun and bow hunters.

However, since once again it is the rutting season which provides the greatest opportunity for archers, it is almost a certainty that high altitude will be part of the story of a successful hunt. Your lungs must adjust to thin air at from 8,000 to 10,000 feet. And, it can get cold in September or October.

Unless you have a resident friend in the state that you plan to hunt, hiring a guide or engaging an outfitter is practically a necessity. Unlike other members of the deer family, with the exception of the caribou, elk are inclined to move over a wide area. Their habits from month to month are governed considerably by weather and insect pests. This means that you must go high in the early part of the season when the rut occurs, or wait and take your chances at the lower elevations after snow has driven them from the heights.

Furthermore, if you try to go it alone or with others of limited experience, you may find yourself surrounded by gunners of like mind. They may keep things stirred up to the extent that you could be spending as much time answering human callers as possibly an elk. A reliable outfitter may be able to get you back into a wilderness area where your chances will be substantially better without so much competition.

Special archery seasons for elk are open in states such as Idaho and Colorado, but it might be well to check these states against the probable rutting season. You may decide that if you can get into a good area where there is little competition from gunners, your chances could be better during the regular firearms seasons.

It is well to make an investigation to determine the background of your outfitter before making any arrangements. Then you should have a complete understanding in writing as to what you might expect from him as well as what equipment you are required to provide on your own. Elk hunts for nonresidents are expensive. And, for many hunters, it may be a once-in-a-lifetime proposition or at least a rare occurrence. You want to get started off right to a good hunt although no one can guarantee the final outcome.

If you have a good guide, calling or bugling for elk will not be your problem. On the other hand, you may wish to get in on the act so that at least you can have the experience of trying to call an elk yourself. At the height of the rut, even the older bulls appear to have trouble distinguishing between a competitor of their own kind and a human faker.

But if you do your own calling, no matter how proficient you might be, you have the problem of getting the animal close enough for a good bow shot. Even if you can make more challenging noises than the elk itself, it might still be best to let your guide do the calling. This will enable you to station yourself somewhere between a responding bull and the caller. This will likely permit you to get much closer shooting than if you try to do the whole job yourself.

If at all possible, it is well to have some means of escape from your shooting position and also some protection there. A love-crazed wapiti can be an extremely dangerous animal, and there are reports of injuries and deaths although I have no record of such involving archers. And, gun hunters are normally shooting at fairly long ranges so that the close proximity of an enraged bull is of little concern.

As with any wild animal, there are no positives relative to their behavior. If you have too much apprehension, it is better to save your money since an archer who substitutes fear for caution is unlikely to be able to make a proper shot at the critical moment. Most wild animals will flee in fright upon first identifying a human. However, if the animal fails to pick up human scent, its actions can be unpredictable.

We are talking about an animal which sometimes stands more than five feet at the shoulder with weights up to about eleven hundred pounds, although the average is much less than this. However, the elk's sharpened antlers provide a most imposing array of lethal spikes that can be extremely dangerous.

Although the chance of a dangerous encounter with an undisturbed elk on the hoof is most unlikely, a wounded animal is an entirely different proposition. Any wild creature should be approached with caution no matter how dead it may appear. Even though a hunter might accidentally be in the way of an elk that has been resting from its wound and decides to lunge forward at human approach, the outcome could be grim.

Cervus canadensis is considered the root species of wapiti, and their former range was primarily from central Canada to northern Mexico. At one time they were found in large areas of the East. Some states still maintain small study herds. The word *elk* is actually a misnomer for this member of the deer family. It is the name given it by Europeans who applied the term used for the moose of the Scandinavian peninsula. For trophy purposes, two elk are recognized by Pope and Young Club competition, the Yellowstone elk and the Roosevelt elk. Yellowstone elk come from the Rocky Mountain states. Oregon and Washington have substantial numbers of Roosevelt elk with most if not all of the record heads coming from the former. Manitoba has a subspecies of the elk and a smaller animal, the Tule wapiti, is found in California. A considerable political flap developed in 1973 over the proposed establishment of a refuge for the some six hundred animals remaining on the West Coast. Conclusion was that the herd is not in danger of extinction and that the state should be permitted to control the destiny of the animals without Federal interference.

Although water transportation is frequently available in remote regions where moose and caribou are found, not so when hunting elk. For this reason alone, because of the animal's huge size, special preparation must be made to get out the carcass of any animal taken. In the early part of the season when the animals are high, packing out a carcass is all but impossible without horses. It is usually when the elk are at lower elevations, or moving down in the less desirable bow hunting period of late fall or early winter, that a do-it-yourselfer has a chance with an off-the-road vehicle.

Today, practically every state and province requires that the meat be brought out. A few men alone without some means of transporting the carcass are in big trouble.

Since the weather governs to some degree the peak of the rutting season, you will simply have to take an educated guess and the chance that goes with it. You must rely on game officials and/or your proposed outfitter to determine the best time for you.

Since it will be a number of months between your application for a license and reservation with an outfitter, you have plenty of chance to get physically in shape for what can be tough going. An occasional visit to the local riding academy is also in order to toughen up those parts that might have to sustain you through a week's hunt up and down over rough trails in a hard saddle.

Here again, know what your license provides and be prepared to take any other game of opportunity for which you may be properly tagged. The additional cost of proper licenses is going to be a fraction of your total cost and might be well worth the investment. This is not intended to discourage anyone from their major objective of taking an elk. Nevertheless, in the event of early success or during those hours when elk are unlikely to be available, you can add other welcome substance to your hunt. There is frequently excellent trout fishing in elk

Snow will eventually drive the elk down from the high places.
(Montana Fish and Game photo by R. Rothweiler)

country. Today's backpack rods, which will accommodate both fly casting or spinning, can provide some momentous hours in between tries for a big bull. Some states provide a combination hunting and fishing license.

When the rut is really on, bulls can frequently be heard at night. However, much as in hunting any of the deer family, your best hours with the bow are from daybreak to about nine or ten o'clock in the morning. Then again in the late afternoon the chances are improved. But, morning is preferred because you have the balance of the day remaining to recover an animal. Since the weather is frequently warm during the middle of the day, elk will move into the heavy timber to rest and to avoid insects.

Your outfitter will undoubtedly try to make it as comfortable as possible for you. However, there are certain hardships that normally go with such a trip. Gripers should stay home since they can ruin the hunt for everybody whether or not game is cooperative. Inconvenience and innovation are common companions to any semi-primitive excursion. They are actually part of the charm of the whole deal if you can accept them in that vein.

Although maximum camouflage is desirable, you may be required to wear blaze orange or some minimum amount of other color if you are hunting in the firearms season. This is one of the things you should check before leaving home on such a trip.

Let the guide know your requirements and limitations, and be sure that he understands exactly your needs. Then, put yourself completely in his hands and take his advice from that point on. If you're not in as good physical shape as you would like to be or if you have any physical drawback whatsoever, be sure to let him know about it. These fellows, in the business for a living, can sometimes be unaware of certain of their guests' limitations. But most will be quite considerate if you are not too embarrassed to tell them about it.

On the other hand, if you have any serious physical problems, you should not chance such a hunt where you are apt to get into serious trouble and foul things up for yourself and all others involved. Even if you have had a good report from your doctor—and a checkup is advisable before such a trip—this does not preclude some illness or health mishap over which you have no control. You can, however, lessen the possibility of such a happening by limiting yourself. Don't be a baby, but don't push yourself beyond your limits.

When you go high on the mountains, you run the risk of being forced down by weather. Or, it is always possible that you can be

For this kind of hunting terrain you should be in good physical condition.

snowed in for days at a time. Even though the days may be warm, it can turn bitterly cold in short order. Because nights are likely to be quite cool, you will need extra clothing for such periods in any event. Hunting is frequently waiting, so you might as well be comfortable while you wait.

A good elk caller can usually tell whether he has a response from a mature bull or a youngster by the sound of the answer. If his lordship answers but refuses to move, he probably has his harem and doesn't want to risk losing any of it by coming to fight with you. Maybe there has been another bull harassing his group. You may have to move closer. But each time your guide stops to call, be sure you have a good vantage point for a shot if it presents itself. Whether you are two or twenty yards from the caller, make certain that you won't be caught away from cover to hide your movements when you make that draw.

And, pick out a single hair on the chest of the elk that you want to hit. Ignore those beautiful antlers. If you choose a particular spot on the animal for your shot and concentrate on it, you may have many years remaining in which to admire those antlers. When you are sure, hold your tension, relax your drawing fingers, follow through. Then, freeze. Stay that way until the animal has left the area.

In the rare (!) instance in which you miss, be very deliberate in putting another arrow on the string if your elk still seems to offer a target. Aim just as carefully, mentally adjusting for the lousy shot you just made, and now do it! That is another reason for the first freeze; you don't want to alarm the quarry in any event. And, it is *possible* that it might stand for a second shot even though the first one scored.

After a hit, give the elk plenty of time before you go on his trail. As with all big animals, the less disturbance the better. With luck, it will not associate its problem with the hunter. But a wounded elk can cover a lot of ground if pushed. It is a heavy animal and a good tracker should have little trouble following its trail even though outward bleeding is sparse.

Remember that all wounded animals, if they do keep going for a time, will eventually head down toward any available water such as a stream or swampy patch. The hunter's key word is *patience*. It is not easy to wait so find something to help pass the time such as whittling a totem, readjusting your boot laces, looking for formations in the clouds, learning the life history of your guide, trying a nap. If possible, give it an hour.

Then move slowly. Keep a watch well ahead of your position on the trail. Antlers are usually first to show on a bull. If you locate the elk, study the situation. It is probably finished; it likely dropped in its death flight. But don't count on it. Treat every carcass as though it is ready to get up running, and prepare accordingly. You have come a long way and worked hard for this moment; don't blow it.

Study the carcass closely for signs of breathing. Keep in mind that an animal downed for a time doesn't require much oxygen; its breathing may be almost imperceptible. If you are quite certain that the animal is dead, make the positive test, preferably with a long stick or your bow tip if nothing better is available. Touch an eye. If it does not flinch, the animal is yours.

Then sit down before you fall down. You should have gallons of adrenalin to work out of your system before you go to work.

Should winter weather set in on the high slopes, it will send the animals down to where they can forage without interference from the weather. During these seasonal migrations it is possible to play the waiting game on well-used trails. Here again the knowledge of an outfitter who has probably lived a considerable part of his life on those slopes in season can place you in the better spots.

Not all elk hunting requires climbing mountains or riding horses. It is not unusual to find elk in good mule deer country in the better states.

Elk and deer sometimes are in season concurrently for bow hunters, and having proper credentials to take either animal can be a decided advantage.

We have moved elk during mule deer drives in Colorado. There are areas where mesas are sufficiently high to provide both elk habitat and fairly easy hunting. There transportation is much less a problem than on the more rugged mountains. In such areas you may also be able to hunt out of a ranch that looks to the hunting season for supplementary income. These are usually private grounds where you have things much to yourself without competition from the hordes of hunters that elk attract during the top weeks of the season on public hunting grounds.

As with moose, the desire is for a trophy head. But where shooting cows is permitted, many hunters will be willing to settle for either a cow or a young bull if the opportunity arises. This is particularly true if meat is a consideration. Those flying in to their hunting may discount the meat as a reward for their excursion, but others may travel to a point of departure in vehicles that will permit bringing home all of the field-dressed carcass.

Because there is so much emphasis on trophy racks, we too often lose sight of the fact that the vast majority of animals taken don't fit anywhere in the record books. The most important factor is what the game kill means to you as a hunter. There have been many times when I have started out full of enthusiasm, filled with dreams of a record head for the bow and arrow, only to be willing in the fading hours of my hunt to take anything legal that comes along. But, there have also been times when I have passed up good shots at legal animals that didn't fit my dreams because I was not in a position to utilize the meat myself. Or, the hour was such that recovery might become a problem because of approaching storm or darkness. So, it can be, too, when hunting for elk.

There is always that time when a man stands alone and is judged only by himself for whatever action he takes or deliberately passes up. There will be those times later when he must live with the meanderings of his conscience and pass personal judgment on his actions. Memories are to be cherished, not to offer bitter reminders.

Depending upon your proximity to good elk hunting territory, you will need about $1,000 in your piggy bank before you are seriously tempted by the enticing photos in the outdoor magazines. The difference in cost between a first-class hunt and a haphazard try to cut corners is not all that much in the overall cost of such a hunt.

You are investing in the possibility of blood-pounding thrills or peaceful periods that are reserved mostly for the gods. Until at last, you may find yourself once above the grandeur upon a high rock, and for that moment, you own it all!

CHAPTER 15

Big Birds

Although it is not anticipated that there is a great following among those who try to take the big birds—turkeys and geese—with the bow and arrow, those with enough dedication should take a look at this specialized sport. Among the feathered targets available to all hunters, these qualify as big game. Although ruffed grouse, ptarmigan, and ring-neck pheasants—even quail—provide their own sport with the bow and arrow, turkeys and geese come under another heading with tackle to fit.

If you think your bow is camouflaged, the bow you use for a big-game animal species, check it again. If there is any shiny surface whatsoever, be sure that it is covered, and that no part of it will reflect sun or even patches of brightness from sky or water. In hunting either of these birds, you must be in good position and be able to move at least a minimum amount if you expect to get good shooting. You don't want your bow to be a giveaway. And, plan to use the same bow that you would use in hunting for the biggest big game for which you are equipped. When we talk about camouflage now, we are up against quarry that are *not* color-blind. There is every evidence that birds distinguish color well. Otherwise, Nature would be playing a gaudy joke by dressing up the male birds of most species in some of the grandest colors to be seen.

Color is not over-emphasized in either the turkey or the goose, but their coloration does stand out amidst natural surroundings. This alone is enough to put these big birds on constant alert since they must instinctively know that the natural adornment which attracts their mates is equally visible to their enemies.

The suggestion here is that arrow fletching be of dull colors. Certainly, no white feathers should be included. If you don't want to change fletching just to hunt birds, then it might be a good idea to spray some dull color such as olive drab or dark car primer on the feathers.

When it comes to arrowheads, the suggestion is that you pay close attention to the broadhead that you plan to use for big birds. Although the previous accent here has been on heads which taper to the shaft in the rear so they will pull free of the shaft without too much difficulty in cases when superficial hits are made on a big-game animal, the heads to be used on the big birds need not provide for such contingency. Rather, the advice is to use a head which is either barbed or cuts off at an abrupt angle to the neck of the head or the shaft. Some bodkin points provide this feature. Since the arrow shaft itself offers a deterrent to the escape of a wounded bird, it is practical to have the head and shaft remain together. This can interfere with wing action in the case of a goose or catch in brush if shot into a turkey.

Above all, the head must be extremely sharp. There is seldom any choice of penetration direction since shots at the big birds will be rare at best. Consequently, the head must be able to penetrate well from any angle. The heavy feathers of a large bird can cause any but the sharpest heads to glance away. A good head alternative is the Wasp, or the Bolo or the Missile Spike. Each has a sharp point or one which can be sharpened for the penetration needed as well as the cutting power required for a good kill.

Although I prefer field points for smaller birds such as grouse and pheasants, the big birds take a lot of arrow impact and you can't go too heavy as long as the arrow is properly balanced. There is a strong possibility that the arrow will stay in the bird in any event since it is difficult to penetrate anywhere in it completely because of the clinging action of flesh and feathers. Using field heads, for example, I was able to take 17 grouse one week on a moose hunt and only two of the arrows passed through. In each latter case, it was a neck shot.

There are two possibilities when hunting geese. One, which involves stalking a flock of birds which are close to shore, or waiting them out on a point or an island where they have been coming in regularly, is a tough way to try. Although waterfowl derive some security from the fact they are out in water, they are still quite sensitive to any noise coming from the land. Further, since the hunter must sooner or later expose at least a part of himself, the chances of his being seen are exactly double the number of birds in the flock. Each pair of eyes is almost continuously alert to unusual movement.

The other possibility is hunting from a regular goose blind, assuming you can find an area where every bush doesn't hide a hunter blasting away at whatever geese come over. In areas where goose hunting is already regulated by number of blinds, you may be able to get a setup where at least you won't be disturbed by nearby gun hunters. In such cases, it is still necessary to know the area thoroughly and where other hunters could be since where the arrows might come down could offer a considerable hazard to other hunters or someone passing by. However, if shooting toward open water there is usually no danger to other than the geese themselves. And this may be considerably less than you would wish it to be.

As in all hunting, it is perfectly fair to take shots where you can get them with the bow. Consequently, even if you want to wait until a goose settles among the decoys, you still have your work cut out for you. Or,

There are occasions when you might get a chance at a single goose.

it might be more appropriate to say that you have a better chance to cut your work out with an arrow.

Whether or not you try to attempt goose hunting and whatever shots you choose, it is all predicated entirely upon just how far you want to try to stretch your luck with the bow and arrow. It is certainly true that Indians took many geese this way. However, in their heyday, waterfowl were considerably less wary than those that come under the guns in this day and age.

There are occasions when you might get a chance for a single goose that has lost its mate or may be recuperating from a gunshot. I recall one particular instance when we were deer hunting, and a Canada goose was spotted in a pasture. Only one of our group had a waterfowl stamp so he had the opportunity all to himself. He managed to approach quite close to this lone goose, but he missed. There didn't appear to be anything particularly wrong with the bird since it took off immediately and flew out over the nearest woods. Occasionally such lone geese will settle on a farm pond or in an area where it is possible to make a try with the bow. Although such chance shots are relatively rare, they may provide the chance to make a stalk to within shooting range.

When it comes to hunting turkeys with the bow and arrow, your best chance by far is during the spring gobbler season, assuming you have the chance to hunt in a state that has one. The best opportunity for a turkey kill with the bow is likely to present itself when the bird is coming to you in response to a call.

In fall hunting, the best chance of calling in birds is after a flock has been broken up by gun shooting. If an archer is along with gunners, an unlikely setup, he then has a fair chance of shooting as the birds respond to a call and begin reassembling. Hence, here we are going to consider only calling gobblers.

Although there are many excellent turkey calls on the market, the only one which lends itself well to hunting turkeys with the bow and arrow is a call such as the Penn's Woods turkey call originated by Roger Latham, outdoor editor for *The Pittsburgh* (Pennsylvania) *Press*. Advantage of this call is the fact that it fits into the roof of the mouth, leaving both hands free to handle the bow. Regardless of the call employed, don't overdo it. Once or twice about every ten or fifteen minutes is usually enough. The turkey will find you without undue coaxing. Anyway, a bad call is apt to alert it or turn it away.

In addition to the seductive perk of the hen turkey, the mouth call can also be used to simulate a gobbler. Some people, unfortunately,

The membrane-type turkey call is good for bow hunters since it leaves both hands free.

with a sensitive gag reflex, aren't able to use a mouth call. For most, however, a bit of practice will produce almost any sounds that are possible with the slate and box calls which have long been on the market.

A variety of other sounds, including crow calls, can also be made with this thin membrane. It is extremely sensitive to proper manipulation with the tongue and vocal chords. The only drawback I have found is the fact that prolonged use will cause its membrane to soften and tear. It also has a tendency to curl and lose its effectiveness if put away while still wet. Consequently, it is well to carry one or two extras which have been "broken in" so that it is possible to switch. Of course, the call could be removed immediately after each use, but this would involve movement which should by all means be avoided. An old gobbler may circle the source of the sound or move in from behind silently. The slightest hunter move could send him on his way.

Of course, the classic response to the artificial call is a healthy gobble, repeated as the old boy heads in to what he anticipates will be a session of love-making. Aside from the squeal and grunt of a bull elk, there are few out-of-door sounds to compare in thrills to that of an amorous tom turkey.

It is not unusual to have turkeys coming in simultaneously or almost so from two or three directions, or to have two or three gobblers moving together from one direction. On one occasion I had two gobblers coming in while a cameraman was hidden with the hope of getting moving pictures of me taking a shot at the turkey with the bow. Unfortunately for our purposes, the two toms came straight at the cameraman and he finally lifted his shotgun practically in self-defense. The gun hit the stump behind which he was hiding, and he missed twice at 14 yards. The distance from where I was calling was only 32 yards, but I couldn't attempt a shot because of the angle of the birds with the cameraman. Had we been in reversed positions, I would have had a rare chance to score. But those are the breaks when you hunt wild turkey with bow and arrow.

I have had birds catch me flat-footed with no place to hide when they responded too soon and came running. On other occasions, I have had gunners deliberately move between me and an answering bird, thus fouling up my chance for a shot.

Although it is natural to seek out spots where the most turkeys are to be found, unless you are hunting private land, it is better to head back into the boondocks to get away from gun competition. There is always a possibility, too, that you will draw turkeys in to some gun

It is not unusual to pull more than one gobbler toward you from the same flock.

hunter who is there properly minding his own business, a case in which it is just a coincidence of circumstance that brings your turkey to him. If you are calling correctly, he has no way of knowing whether you are the real thing or another caller. He would be foolish to pass up an opportunity that comes all too seldom, even with the gun.

So there you have it. Just getting a shot at either of the big birds— goose or turkey—poses handicaps and improbabilities that are almost overwhelmingly adverse for anyone serious about trying to score. And, trying to make a hit on what is a relatively small target when compared to other species of big game, is itself another obstacle to success.

Still, the outdoor situations under which you might have a chance to score are certain to bring other thrills. These often transcend the one of merely counting coup on old ugly-head sauntering through the woods, acting much like a juvenile in a new suit passing some soda fountain lined with girls. Or, if it is one of Nature's winged noblemen dropping in out of the fog to brake over a collection of deceitful decoys, memory of the moment will hang its own trophy in the mind of the archer bold enough to try, whatever the outcome.

CHAPTER **16**

Pigs

Within the U. S. our only claim to having a native wild pig is tied to the collared peccary, commonly known as the javelina, for which hunting is found only in the states of Texas, Arizona and New Mexico. This is rather a long reach since the peccary is in a class by itself even though some authorities believe that pigs and peccaries are descended from the same ancestor some 55 million years ago. True pigs, on the other hand, are all descended somewhere along the line from animals which originated in Europe and India. There are no truly native North American pigs. However, since eating habits and general habitat of peccaries, wild boars and feral pigs are so similar, we will view them together for bow hunting purposes.

At one time the peccary was threatened with extinction after market hunters drove it from as far north as the Red River in Arkansas into the hunting range it presently occupies. In 1938 a game survey showed fewer than 44,000 animals. As with all game animals, however, the peccary today is in little danger of extinction due to protective game laws. Since a female produces normally but one shoat a year compared to from four to six by feral pigs in the wild state, close regulation is necessary to perpetuate the species.

Because peccaries will feed on anything, from acorns to carrion, trying to pinpoint their feeding location at a given time can be difficult. It is well to hunt with someone familiar with your chosen area so that you will at least be in favorable territory. Hunting tackle need not be overly sophisticated since a really big boar peccary will not go over 75 pounds. The average is considerably less than this. As in all big-game hunting, however, it is important to make a good hit.

Pugnacious qualities and sharp tusks are reasons enough to make a killing shot since a wounded peccary can be a rough customer to handle. However, there is little or nothing to fear from these gregarious animals that usually travel in herds of about a dozen. In areas of good food, larger herds may be encountered. The big problem for the archer is trying to get close to them rather than entertaining any fear towards the reverse. A cornered peccary will threaten, but it is most unlikely to attack a human.

With dogs it is different, as many well-scarred hounds could testify. Although the tusks are small compared to those of true pigs, only one-and-a-half to two-inches long, they are extremely sharp. The two upper and two lower tusks are well hidden by grooves in the snout.

Peccaries may frequently be located by scent since the strong musk gland located on its back will give away the animal's general location if

The collared peccary, or javalina, is a favorite of bow hunters in the Southwest.

it is moving upwind. And, it is important to stalk it upwind, for this animal's sense of smell is highly developed. Frequently the archer's only evidence of javelina is their sound running through the brush. Smaller specimens provide the best eating, but with all it is necessary to remove the musk gland immediately to avoid its affecting the meat.

Available to more archers and becoming increasingly popular are wild relatives of once domesticated Spanish pigs in Florida and Georgia. Even older than the wild ancestors of once tame pigs in the Southeast are tuskers of the Hawaiian Islands, believed to have been brought there by the early settlers sometime after A.D. 400. It is known that Captain Cook brought English pigs to the Islands as early as 1778. But wherever the domestic pig has turned back to its wild state, it becomes a quarry worthy of the archer's best hunting talent and principles of sportsmanship.

Pig hunting has survived from classical times although much of history combines dogs and spears in the pursuit of pigs. This sport undoubtedly evolved because of the courageous nature of the animal. It will frequently stand and fight because of its limited power of locomotion. Particularly where the domestic animal reverted to the wild state many years ago, it is far removed from the sloppy barnyard swine most commonly thought of. In the wild state the pig is a fairly clean and wary creature. At one time it was actually used in England to point game, which should be a clue to its highly developed powers of scent.

Bring on your heaviest tackle for these feral creatures. And be prepared to have an avenue of escape such as a good climbing tree, if you only wound one of them. Although they do not have the layers of fat common to domestic swine, it takes a good hit in the heart or lungs to bring a pig down. They will charge when cornered or wounded, and the heavy tusk armament can inflict serious and even fatal injuries.

On the Hawaiian Islands the sport has survived for many years, with dogs used to drive the pig to bay. Then the intrepid natives move in with knives and attempt to cut the throat. At least one human death in hunting them has been reported. Also, there was an instance in which a hunter had the ligaments ripped in both wrists when he moved in on a pig that had taken refuge in a cave under tree roots.

I participated in such a hunt with wildlife biologist Jon Giffin, formerly of Utah, who was completing a four-year live study of feral pigs in the rain forests for the game department on the island of Hawaii. The game would be brought to bay by dogs. Then Jon and Milton Kealoha, his assistant, would put a rope on the pigs, wrestle them to the ground, take blood samples, and ear-tag them. Jon carried a pistol, but in taking

Feral pigs of this size require the heaviest in bow hunting tackle.

over one thousand pigs he was never forced to use it. Nevertheless, it was a hairy business.

On our last of four pigs of the day, a nasty black boar, I suddenly found myself the object of its rage, protected only by two cameras and, fortunately, two dogs. The boar had just been tagged and released. Normally, the pigs would take off, but this one decided to stand and fight. I was caught in the open and each time the pig would lunge my way, one of the dogs would force it back. Jon, safe on the high trunk of a fallen tree, answered my question about what my best move should be.

"Whatever you do, be positive!"

I took *positive* aim at some vines along a high bank and was about to make a run for it when the dogs got the boar moving in the opposite direction.

Archery clubs sometimes purchase captive pigs from Florida or Georgia which are given cholera inoculations at least 21 days before being released for local hunting. This insures that they will not spread disease in the event that they are not taken and eventually breed with domestic stock. Probably the best known of these hunts is one at Forksville, Pennsylvania, where a bow hunters' festival is held each September. Up to 16 of the feral porkers are released and as many as 250 bow hunters make a try for them. Some of these animals go over 200 pounds and are really formidable quarry. More than one archer has been sent up a tree by the provoked pigs.

On the Hawaiian Islands, the feral pigs are treated as other wild game although the season is usually open the year around for archers. The use of dogs is permitted in some areas.

The only true wild boar in the United States are the offspring of several brought to this country by an Englishman named George Moore who released them in 1910 in North Carolina. Since these pugnacious pigs feed mainly at night, chances of getting one on a wait or by stalking them are difficult. Traditionally, as in Europe, the wild boars are hunted with dog packs. They are considered a real challenge even to a gun hunter, who is encouraged to use a heavy, high-powered rifle for them. These descendants of the true wild boar, *Sus scrofa* are considerably more dangerous than any other animal in North America with the exception of the grizzly and polar bear. These tuskers will sometimes charge a hunter on sight if aggravated by a pack of dogs.

A bow hunter seeking these animals, which are reported to weigh up to 600 pounds and are commonly killed at 350 pounds, would do well to make positive plans. The head of either a wild or a feral tusker is a most impressive wall trophy although the manner of taking it may depend more upon the skill of the dogs than that of the archer. However, the element of danger does make seeking the wild boar potentially one of the most exciting of all hunts.

All pigs, whether feral or wild, have the ability to absorb a tremendous amount of punishment before going down. Even then, considerable caution should be used in approaching a pig that has been shot. Any are capable of inflicting painful or serious injuries.

Although the word *pig* has many connotations which are not favorable to the animal in general, none of them apply to either the feral or the wild animal. They are extremely courageous, ferocious, and tough.

The true, wild, variety can run for long distances at speeds that are almost unbelievable. Although it will normally flee at the sight of man

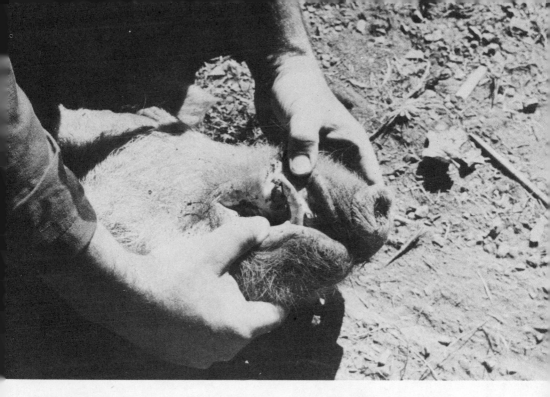

Tusks like these are capable of inflicting serious injury to the careless bow hunter.

or dog, when it tires of running it is a most formidable adversary to man or beast. Range of the wild boar is largely confined to lower Tennessee, North Carolina, a small section of South Carolina and Northern Georgia.

Feral pigs are found chiefly in such diverse spots as the contiguous states of Florida and Georgia, and the Hawaiian Islands.

Their extremely destructive habits will likely continue to restrict their range, but the respect of those who hunt them with the bow and arrow will forever continue to increase.

CHAPTER 17

Predators

There was a time, not too many years ago, when any of the big predators were considered more bad than good. They were open season everywhere all year around. Today, because of the effort to maintain an ecological balance, it is necessary to check up on local game laws to determine whether or not you can legally loose an arrow at these targets of opportunity or to make specific hunts for them.

Random examples show that the wildcat is now fully protected throughout the year in Pennsylvania. Alaska has seasons on the wolf in certain areas, cougars are being regarded as big game in some of the western states and a hard look is being taken by others. The only major predators common to many of the states which are not generally given protection, to my knowledge, are the fox and the coyote. Each of these has managed to survive despite every effort to control their numbers and whether protected or not. Nonresident hunters, especially, should check the laws of the locality or the state in which they plan to hunt since there is no guarantee that either or both may be legally hunted.

Certainly it is not to be implied from the preceding that this writer is against protecting these creatures where it is deemed advisable. In fact, it is my personal hope that none of the predators will ever become extinct anywhere in the country. Moreover, I consider it a privilege to share in the harvest of edible species that rightfully belong first to those creatures created to maintain a proper ecosystem anywhere in the world.

It is a natural coincidence, however, that these predators are most likely to be found in areas where there is generally good big-game hunting. To many hunters a wolf would be much more a trophy, where permitted, than the moose or the deer upon which it feeds on occasion. But I would be just as pleased with a photo if there was any threat to the continued existence of whatever species of predators I might happen to be hunting.

There have been shot opportunities. There was a comical situation on a deer hunt in New York one fall when a red fox went down a dirt road ahead of me, completely unaware of my existence. A careful stalk finally revealed the red fellow digging for mice in a woodland meadow. My arrow must have barely nicked it where it sat, for the fox's tail went straight up in the air. It remained erect as the red tore across the meadow and road to disappear in the woods. On another occasion, a red fox had apparently been bedded near where I moved in to await deer at the edge of a pasture. It was only 15 feet away, tiptoeing toward other cover, but hemlock boughs prevented a try for it with the bow.

A coyote presented an opportunity in Colorado when it came loping up the canyon at the head of a deer drive. Expecting that it would bolt at the first movement, I made a try at 20 yards and was a fraction low with my arrow. However, the coyote never changed speed nor direction and within seconds was no more than ten feet from me on its way out of the canyon.

A black timber wolf, so close that silver tips on its fur were visible, trotted in near a moose stand in Quebec one day at no more than 50 yards distance. My hunting companion was carrying a rifle, and when he leveled on the animal, I figured the show was all but over and started to unlimber my camera. In his excitement, the gun hunter missed three standing shots as the wolf moved around some old stumps in the swamp. He blasted two more as the big fellow streaked across the swamp grass after finally figuring it was high time to get out of there.

Targets of opportunity are sometimes the frosting on a hunt that may or may not produce the intended quarry. Frequently, such opportunities are so unexpected that the chance to score is much less than when deliberately seeking out such animals. It is rare that an archer will score under such circumstances, but just the opportunity to try can provide the highlight to any trip.

Where permitted, electronic fox calls can produce action under a controlled setup which is quite likely to be productive. Recordings of actual foxes in distress, rabbit squeals and assorted other sounds which create interest or ring the dinner bell for foxes can be especially effective. On occasion, foxes have been known to pounce right on the machine itself. Grays are much more apt to respond to the artificial call than the better educated reds. Use of a headlamp with the lens covered by red cellophane or tinted to produce a red light seems to have little effect on the foxes during the hours of darkness when they are most apt to be out hunting. Also, at night the air is more likely to be still and without any movement of human scent which too often otherwise provides a barrier that no fox wants to risk crossing.

In the western part of the country, the coyote can be fooled in much the same manner. Artificial mouth calls can be equally effective when used by someone who is knowledgeable about coyotes. As with all bow hunting, the archer frequently must take satisfaction from just the opportunity rather than a score. It is difficult enough to take game in the daytime, but night shooting requires much more alertness and coordination between eye and arm.

It is never really easy to call in foxes, cats, or coyotes. Success will be somewhat dependent upon the number of predators available, how hungry or curious they are, and whether or not they have been tricked before. Generally, the hunter's movement is more apt to foul up shooting than any other factor. When a predator comes to call, it is intent upon finding the source of the sound, and all its aggressive instincts will be on edge. The animal's concentration can work to the advantage of the bow hunter if he stations himself in an advantageous location away from the call, whether it is electronic or a companion utilizing a mouth call. Nevertheless, it is well to have the source of the sound within bow range. Predators sometimes come swiftly in to attack the supposedly injured rabbit or to defend another of its kind. Of course, care must be taken not to shoot in the direction of another hunter, particularly in the sudden excitement that appearance of another predator can produce. This in itself is reason enough to have a good view of the likely area of action.

At other times, the animal may come skulking in, actually stalking the source of the call, whether it is man or machine.

It goes without saying that many predators approach without ever being seen. They either become suspicious because of the call itself or pick up the scent of those lying in wait. This is another good reason to locate yourself as far away from the source of the sound as you feel is

Where legal, electronic calls are a great aid in bringing in predators.

still within scoring range. This should also give you an equal distance beyond to cover in the event the predator is reluctant or suspicious, and hangs back on the fringes.

Even though an electronic call is not utilized in your hunt, it might be well to listen to one beforehand and practice mouth call. There are those who can make vocal sounds which closely simulate natural sounds. However, most must depend upon an artificial assist.

The ability to remain motionless until the moment of shooting cannot be overemphasized. Otherwise you may be bringing in animals that you never see because they see you first. Or, you can foul up your own opportunities simply because you lose faith in the caller. Even though the call ceases, whether human or electronic, remain still for a reasonable time. It is always possible that an animal coming in will become even more excited by the ensuing absence of sound. An extra fifteen minutes is not too long to wait.

Both the source of the call and the hunter should be in a position where neither can be easily spotted. Aside from preventing the animal from seeing the hunter, the concealment afforded by brush will sometimes enable the archer to draw without being observed. If an animal is spotted coming in and it seems determined to continue its course and there is no air movement, it is best to let it pass your stand, if possible. Predators have best forward vision and you may be able to draw your bow without being observed even though you cannot remain completely hidden during the process.

In the use of an electronic caller, which involves a tape or a record, it is well to listen to it over and over so that you know about what to expect. Don't do as one of my sons and I did one day on a trip for crows. We had everything well set up, we thought, and I turned on the machine and scurried back to my planned hiding place. The record came on with an excellent rendition of a flock of angry crows, and things both looked and sounded fine. Then the message hesitated, and the next sound blared out something like this: "Good afternoon fellow sportsmen!"

Inadvertently I had picked up an instruction record rather than a regular call. Both of us burst out laughing and I am sure that any crows attracted to the initial chorus must have done the same.

Almost impossible to call is the wary timber wolf. My own experience on this is most limited. In the one instance in which a wolf came in to our hunting stand, it is possible that previous moose calls may have brought it in. Prior to this happening we had been hearing wolves for two days and this may also have been why no moose had shown. There were actually three wolves approaching our stand, but two of them ducked into the bush before the big fellow came along to provide shooting for my companion with a gun. Whether he would have approached close enough for a good bow shot I will never know, but even at an estimated 50 yards there was an outside chance that I may have been able to score with an arrow.

With a pack of excellent hounds, cougar hunts are frequently elaborate and expensive setups. It is simply a case of following the dogs until an animal is treed. Then the archer needs only to find an opening with the hope of bringing the cat down. It is little different than hunting the big cats with the gun, a matter of individual stamina rather than individual hunting ability. The biggest problem is in getting the animal up a tree where it will stay put long enough to afford a shot. Otherwise, the whole procedure starts all over again and it can be a long day trying to finish off the cat.

One consideration in such hunting is the possibility of a dog being injured by an arrowhead projecting from or in the quarry's carcass. A properly sharpened broadhead can be dangerous to a hound that is terribly excited and interested only in getting a bite of the action. For this reason some raccoon dog handlers will hold or tie their animals during bow shooting until it is determined that there is no danger to the dogs before they are freed to worry the carcass.

Plenty of practice should be taken beforehand since nearly vertical shooting is somewhat different than shooting on the level. You will find, through practice, that your hold on target is somewhat higher than when shooting on a level plane. It can be both embarrassing and frustrating to find that you have difficulty scoring on what would normally seem to be a fairly easy shot. Also, there is the matter of expensive arrows to consider since the recovery rate on shafts shot at a high angle is not good. Further, in the usual cat country, arrows frequently come down on hard rock and are hardly worth recovering even if they can be found.

Since bow hunting problems are somewhat magnified in predator hunting, the question might arise: "Why bother in the first place when a gun is so much more efficient?" To a dedicated bowhunter the answer is the same as when he hunts for anything with his primitive arm. Predators are not so scarce that a kill with an arrow is going to make much difference in the total ecology of a given area, in any event.

If there is a real problem, and destruction of the predator is considered a necessity, then it is probably best to go with the gun to do the job. On the other hand, where predators are plentiful, they should provide great bow hunting!

Probably the greatest attraction in hunting predators is the fact that with probably few exceptions they are usually available all year around under the law. It is an off-season challenge that is most demanding of the archer and his tackle. So, if you are interested but have no one available who has had previous experience, check the archery magazines for calls, instructions and any other information you can gather on the side.

Whether you simply take a target of opportunity, or make a dedicated study of hunting predators with the bow and arrow, there is a genuine thrill as roles are reversed and the hunter becomes the hunted. You, as a predator, are in reality simply asserting your rights among other predators. After all, they are your competitors for the right to share in the harvest of edible game species.

Man-made laws govern our main activities, but for the most part, when we seek predators we become subject to natural law. Nevertheless, we must accept the fact that our need is never so great as that of our competition.

All of the previous is one way to attempt to put it objectively. But if each of us is subjectively honest, we must admit that predator hunting is also just another way to justify our pleasure in the great game of hunting with the bow and arrow.

CHAPTER 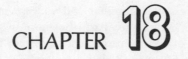 18

Water Ways

There are certain seasons of the year when there really is nothing much to hunt with the bow and arrow in the way of either game or predators. From spring to late summer, most game is out of season and it is too hot to hunt anyway. With one exception. If you rig up properly and go to the right places, there is big game in both fresh and salt water that will test the mettle, and to an extent, the shooting ability of any archer.

Until you have experienced the violence of ramming a fishhead through the tough skin of a shark, battled against the power of a big stingray, tested your nerve against an alligator gar, or tried to deter the determination of a big carp impaled on an arrow, you are missing out on some of the most interesting sport to be found anywhere. And at least one of these creatures can be found just about anywhere, the carp.

How you go about it will largely determine how much sport you get out of it. Frequently that is all you will get out of it since none of the fish named is considered worthy of space in the deep-freeze when it comes to eating. However, their removal from the waters, if not a blessing, certainly will not upset the balance of Nature in the numbers taken by bow and arrow hunters.

Since the carp is most familiar and widespread across the country, this is a good place to start as it will be more available to the average bow hunter. Carp, of course, can range anywhere from a few ounces to real lunkers in the fifty-pound and up class. Since small carp can be taken on archery tackle that might be used for any kind of trash fish, let's confine our thoughts here primarily to the bigger ones that test both the bowman's hunting ability and skill.

Regardless of what type of fish one goes after, there are three approaches. The initial shot, which is most important, is the same in all cases. Immediately after the arrow strikes a fish, you can play it three ways. One, and the more common, is simply to use line strong enough so that the fish can be played in hand-over-hand. The other is to use an arrangement whereby the fight is transferred to a rod and reel connected to the archery tackle so that the fish can then be played the conventional way. But, there is the third way.

Many years ago, carp shooting so fascinated me that I put a good deal of thought into it with the desire to increase the sporting aspects. Whether it was a *first* or not, it was an original idea, at least locally, to attach a spinning reel directly to the back of the bow. The line from this reel was attached to the fishhead. Sometimes we would run the line up the shaft and anchor it lightly near the nock with a piece of tape or rubberband so that the line would better follow the arrow. Of course, it was necessary to open the bail on the reel. When spincast reels became popular, they were even better since they eliminated the chance of the monofilament becoming caught on the bail itself. Everything depends, of course, upon the ability to remember that the reel must be set so that the line can run freely at the shot. Although we dreaded what might happen if this was forgotten, the chance came soon enough to discover that it did no more than break the line and foul up the shot.

In this manner, the fish can be played from the reel somewhat as with a fishing rod. This is still an ideal setup for carp although it becomes a bit strenuous when you whack into a really big one. It is one that works well whether shooting from a boat or stalking fish along shore using the hip boot routine.

The alternative is to fasten the bow line from a regular bow reel directly to the line from a set-up rod and reel, allowing enough slack so that there is no drag at the shot. This is primarily for boat hunting. Assuming a hit, it is a simple matter to lay the bow down and grab the fishing rod to play the carp in the conventional manner. A carp is not a spectacular fighter, but its long powerful sweeps up and down the river or around the lake provide action with an uncertain outcome and gives

Carp are the most widespread fish targets for bow hunters across the country.

all the zest found in catching these fish in the normal way. In fact, the carp has considerably more power when it is impaled in the tail area or even forward in the body since it has not nearly as good leverage when hooked in the mouth. It is only when the fish is shot in the spine and turns its belly that the archer is denied the thrilling battle which comes with a sizeable fish.

The average carp is in the four- to six-pound class, and even these give a fair account of themselves. However, knowledge of where the big ones wallow can up this average by many pounds. Anything over 15 pounds is a tough customer on a rod and reel. Normally, the wound created by a fishhead driven by an arrow initially causes the fish little more trouble than a hook. The trouble is more likely to occur in the boat or along the shore, depending upon which method is used to seek out targets.

A variation in carp hunting is to go at night. By drifting downstream with the current or rowing slowly over the shallows, you can frequently spot bigger fish. The light may be a powerful gas-fed beam which shoots down into the water. Or a simple gooseneck lamp arrangement powered by a 12-volt wet cell can be constructed to illuminate an area perhaps six to eight feet in diameter. Once the light is submerged, it can be turned on and it will not be affected by the cold water. However, any attempt to first switch on the light and then submerge it will invariably result in a broken bulb.

Since at best the area that will be illuminated will be relatively small, shooting must be fast. Under artificial light carp appear gray in the water and they are easily distinguishable from game fish. When a big one is hit, it is an eerie sensation to play against the power tugging at your rod or hands somewhere out there in the darkness. Occasionally a big carp will ram the boat or pass under it to create all kinds of excitement and confusion.

Since shooting is normally close and accuracy is not so much a problem as in normal hunting, we frequently use junk wooden arrows with the head fitted loosely so that the shaft will disengage after the hit is made. Commercial solid glass arrows will penetrate the water much better, but they are too expensive to expend the shaft and you must go all the way with them. They do create a drag on the fish which is certain to cut down its fighting ability.

Commercial bow reels come in many sizes and shapes. Most are made so that they can be taped fast to the riser section of modern bows. Some permit shooting through the center of an oversized rig which allows the heavy line—from 50 to 80 pounds—to run freely from the reel after the hit. These are strong enough to handle a large fish although cuts in water-softened hands are common if a big one is impaled. The same rig can also be utilized with a fishing rod by having the end of the line which would normally be fastened to the bow reel, attached to a fishing line running from a rod. The bow *reel* is actually a glorified spool on which line is wrapped by hand since it has no moving parts.

Since it is a problem in all bow shooting at underwater objects, refraction must be taken into consideration. Technically, refraction is a deflection from a straight path undergone by light when passing from one medium into another in which its velocity is different. This is what makes an oar or a stick appear to jut off under water on a different angle at the point where it enters the water. This visual distortion is of some moment to the archer trying to hit an object under the water since it will always be closer than it appears to be. If the fish is near the surface or in the shallows, this presents no great problem, particularly if it is a large fish. The error may be so slight that the arrow will still find flesh. However, since the desire is to make a good solid hit in the meaty part on a fish, it is always necessary to aim somewhat below the intended point of impact.

This bow reel permits both aiming and shooting through its center.

There is also undoubtedly some deviation in the straight line created by impact at an angle into the water to further raise the true path of the arrow from that at which it cuts the surface of the water.

Since it is difficult to determine the angle, or even the distance below the water where you want the arrow to hit, adjusting correctly for refraction comes only with practice. Just keep in mind that the shallower the angle of the arrow, and the deeper the fish lies in the water, the greater will be the need to correct for refraction. For instance, on the occasional shot straight down under the boat, there is no need to make any correction. Refraction increases with the angle from the perpendicular as well as depth of the fish simply because you are looking through more water. In murky or muddy water, this is of little account since the fish seen must necessarily be fairly close to the surface. In clear water, refraction can be much more a problem since it will tempt you to make shots that are all but impossible. Any trout fisherman who has tried to wade what appeared to be a shallow riffle, and then ended up with two boots full of water, is quite aware of this visual distortion.

When it comes to arrowheads for big fish, there is a bit of a problem. The ideal head is one which unscrews so that the barb can be reversed and the arrow pulled completely from the fish after it is captured. Single, or even double heavy wire barbs impede the head's penetration into a big fish and simply won't cut through the tough hide of anything such as a shark. The best head I have found for all-around big-fish shooting on underwater targets is the Sting-a-ree. This is a heavy duty head with collapsible double barbs one and three-eighths inches long. These will work "as is" on a soft fish such as carp, but both the head and the forward curve on the barbs should be sharpened with a file when attempting to take big stingrays or sharks. The barbs can be reversed simply by twisting the shaft with the head held rigid.

For fast and sure shooting, the spawning season of the carp, which occurs in most areas in early May, provides the maximum in excitement. This does not usually bring the bigger carp, however, and these fellows must frequently be stalked back in the sloughs with utmost care. They got big by being wary, and a careless approach will many times produce no more than a huge wake as the monsters charge out into deep water. A hit under such circumstances would be loaded with luck.

Even when carp are not spawning—and spring floods can foul up the spawn sport by discoloring the water—they can be stalked anytime in the shallows early and late like any other game. At daybreak, and until the sun hits the water, carp can frequently be found by looking for mud streaks or movement among the reeds and grass along shore. Where it is possible to wade along shallow streams or hunt from the bank, these telltale signs will quite often locate carp for you. Or, simply by standing quietly at a point of land or a shallow channel between two islands, good shooting may result. Toward evening, carp will again return to such spots after cruising in deep water or resting during the brighter hours of the day. The same procedure can be followed with a boat along the shores where backwaters and sloughs provide ideal carp shooting opportunities.

Most states require a fishing license for such activities. Consequently, although best carp shooting comes at best fishing hours, you may be letting yourself in for a lot of extra sport by rigging your bow for carp on your next fishing excursion during the warm months.

Shooting stingrays follows much the pattern of activity in hunting carp. These monstrous flat fish frequent shallow bays and hang around clam beds where they are most unwelcome. There are numerous variations of these flattened sharks such as the skates, sawfishes, guitarfishes, leopard rays and giant mantas or devilfish.

But, stingrays of fifty pounds and up to nearly three hundred pounds will provide sufficient excitement wherever they are found. When spawning, their huge, flattened shapes are seen as splotches of brown which can come alive with explosive force after an arrow finds them. Nothing but the heaviest tackle should be used since, as with carp, these fish are quite capable of pulling a rather large boat around before they are subdued. When stingrays in the seventy to one hundred-pound class decide to take off, there is little that can stop them until they poop out and permit you to bring them to boat.

Even then they really should be handled carefully since lethal stingers projecting from the body about one-third of the tail length can cause a painful wound at best and death at the worst. The rays should be brought over the side inverted so that they can't whip their tails around until the stingers are cut loose from them. One ray in the ninety-pound class that I took off Chincoteague, Virginia had a double stinger.

Pursuing rays in clear water such as is found in the Florida Keys is an exhilarating sport and the old problem of refraction becomes a real handicap. If you are tempted to try for one of the huge eagle rays or leopard rays that abound in the shallows off the Keys, more power to you, but plan for a long arduous fight and a big question mark over the outcome. In any saltwater bow hunting, it might be well to use a long length of wire leader.

Wire is a must for sharks since their abrasive skin can wear through anything less. The sanest sport is to seek out smaller sharks up

Combining the bow and fishing rod on big stingrays provides plenty of excitement.

Clear water of the Florida Keys provides problems in refraction.

to one hundred pounds in the shallows such as blacktips, lemons, and sand sharks. My most ambitious try was off Pensacola with Dennis Majewski, veteran shark fisherman despite his relative youth. We used up several hundred pounds of bonita trying to bring a shark to the surface without success.

But when this failed, a six-pound bonita was impaled on a couple shark hooks and dropped over the side. It was only a short time until the bait started moving and Dennis put the hooks to the shark with all his strength. He then muscled the fish up to within about four feet of the surface and I managed to get a broadhead into it.

The commotion which followed left all of us exhausted. We were locked in with a hammerhead that measured over ten feet and weighed 174 pounds. As we worked it to the surface, the shark started to roll and soon had both lines well wrapped around it. This inhibited its thrashing, but it was not until another archer drew blood with a broadhead that the big one quieted down enough so a rope could be put on it. It was too big to get into the boat, and we had to tow it to shore, some several miles, to weigh and measure it.

It was necessary to team up on this hammerhead shark.

In fresh or brackish water, gar provide excellent sport. And, in the case of alligator gar, considerably more than that. Smaller gar are not too hard to find although they are difficult to hit because of their slender outline. Alligator gar, which will go two hundred pounds or better and measure as much as ten feet in length, offer the ultimate in freshwater action. These Sunny South leviathons are sometimes found on the surface where they come up for air, and the sharpest, biggest fishhead possible is needed to penetrate their thick scales and hide.

As with all really big fish, they are extremely wary and just trying to get close to one is quite a venture. The nearest I came to a shot at one was late evening on a Florida lake where a gar of two hundred pounds-plus had been reported. We didn't actually see the thing. But in the dusk we must have come close, because a sudden swirl that rocked our heavy boat gave us every reason to believe that we had come within shooting distance of a target that would have probably kept us busy well into the hours of darkness.

In all such fish hunting, with the possible exception of the carp, there is strong element of danger. Anyone desiring to match wits and muscle with these sometimes pugnacious creatures that have survived little change in millions of years should be prepared to fight them in *and* out of the water. Make no mistake, there are additional risks in finally capturing such monsters. It is sport for sport's sake. These fish range from low on the scale of edibility down to zero. A heavy club or a pistol can be of help in subduing the larger and more dangerous of the lot before attempting to boat them or putting a tow rope on them.

An alternate way of trying to play such fish immediately after the hit is similar to the method of jugging a catfish. Rather than anchoring the end of the line to which the fish arrow is attached, a white detergent bottle or large bobber is sometimes used. After a hit is made, the float with the line attached is tossed over the side to be picked up later. It then becomes a hand-over-hand proposition in retrieving the fish. But, always, a gaff or an oversized landing net should be available if the catch is of such size that it will fit into the net.

To most, such bow hunting has many unfamiliar aspects. It is well to go first with someone who has had some experience to reduce the element of danger associated with this activity. By all means carry a belt knife readily available in the event that you or someone becomes tangled in a line that can cause painful cuts or actually drag a person overboard. When hunting large sharks, a second boat should be available since these pea-brained monsters will sometimes smash into a boat containing their tormentors. This is big-game hunting where the quarry frequently fights back, and it is never counted dead until it is hanging on block and tackle or sinks into the deep with its belly slit.

If you spill most of your first drink after such a trip, anyone who has bowhunted for the waterway big ones will understand.

Shooting fish is off-season sport of the finest kind. Whether you mix it up with harmless carp or saltwater brutes that can kill you, this is

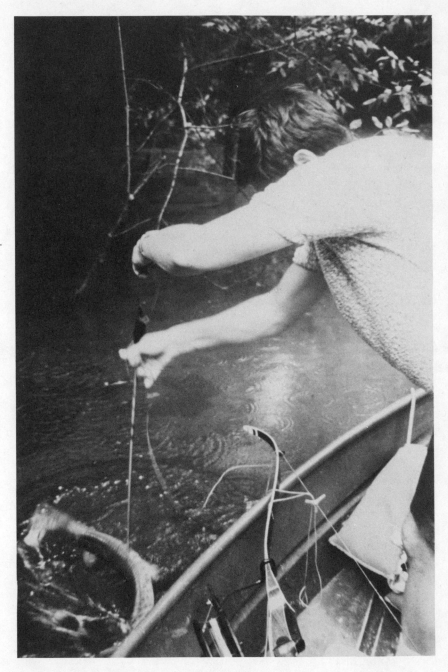

Gar are just another of the aquatic targets which entice bowmen.

big-game hunting in every sense. True, it is intended to result in the death of a creature with not even the excuse of needing food. Like varmint hunting, however, it permits the hunter to salve any sympathy he might have for the victim with the knowledge that he is ridding the environment of an undesirable inhabitant.

Although permitted in salt water and in some states, this writer is opposed to the shooting of any game fish with the bow and arrow. As one who alternates for sport between hunting and fishing seasons, I shudder at the thought that an archer might kill a fish that deserves to test its strength against a fishing rod. Even worse, it might deprive some hopeful of a potential angling record.

But, whether you stand poised on the prow of a boat or pick your way in waders through the shallows to challenge creatures that can test the heaviest combinations of archery and fishing tackle, you are truly in a contest. Perhaps, with the exception of seeking the big land carnivores, bow hunting the waterways puts you closer to par with the intended quarry than any other hunting sport. Don't miss out on it.

CHAPTER 19

Wrap Up

At this point, there is the hope that we have come closer together in our approach as well as our feelings toward this revived sport of bow hunting. For, as bow hunters, we are inseparably joined in our desire and our privilege. A special handclasp goes to those gunners who may be taking their first look at archery as a hunting sport or who may already count it as an extra way to participate.

As the population expands, we will be running into each other more and more. And, we must share the same calumet. There are far too many today who would deprive us, gunners and archers, of the heritage that stems as much from instinct as from deliberate desire to participate.

We must, however, deserve the rights that we have taken unto ourselves through the succession of homo sapiens from the dark caves of the prehistoric unknown to the cloudy horizon of today. A disgusting minority that has invited criticism of gun hunting has crept also into the expanding army of archers. It is an unfortunate truism that all hunters are not sportsmen. However, neither are all athletes, nor politicians, nor preachers nor used-car salesmen—honest. There are rules governing the conduct of each because they are collectively people.

Nevertheless, the bow hunter implies by his adoption of a primitive arm that he has taken a step above the pulsating plane of common human behavior. He trades less strenuous routes to pleasure for the more difficult. It would seem as though these facts alone would mark him as a person deserving the name of *sportsman*. Unfortunately, it sometimes isn't so.

Numerous game wardens I have talked to are generally pleased with the conduct of bow hunters. Some admitted to early misgivings when archery came on stronger but changed their attitude. This is all to the good.

Vermont stepped out in 1968 with a provision that archers could participate in the special bow hunting season, take any one deer, and again hunt with bow or gun in the following regular firearms season for antlered deer. Archery licenses increased 75% over the previous year, but the percentage of success varied little. A questionnaire was distributed to determine results as well as type of tackle used since there are few restrictions.

It was found that hunters naturally chose tackle which increased their possibilities. For example, only a few reported using bows of less than 31 pounds and none using these were successful. A number had kills with bows in the 31 to 40-pound class, but the greatest success ratio came in the 41 to 50-pound class. Most used fiberglass shafts with arrowheads of more than two blades. Overall success ratio was 6.6%— high for the Northeast. General satisfaction was expressed by the Vermont Fish and Game Department with the experiment. The arrangement has been continued with results somewhat similar based upon available deer. This northern state's deer population fluctuates with the severity of winter weather.

This example, although further studies are planned, illustrates that bow hunting can be improved by open-minded game officials if general hunter behavior is satisfactory. It is one way to harvest animals which might be sacrificed on the highways while generating revenue which works to the benefit of all hunters and wildlife lovers. Reduction of the deer herd before the gunning season is insignificant. In Vermont, a four-year study under the liberalized regulations showed that 38.9% of deer taken in the early archery season were fawns, or deer of the year; 39.5% were adult does; and 21.6% were adult bucks.

Wisconsin continues to produce the highest number of deer taken by bow hunters with a success ratio of about 7%. In 1972, a total of 7,085 deer were taken, and the annual bow hunter harvest has ranged between 6,000 and 7,500 since 1966. Record take of whitetails in the nation was established in Wisconsin in 1967 when 7,592 were reported.

The amount of misinformation on the subject of bow hunting which gets into print is unfortunate. Because of divergent views, not all editors will agree. But there are few who are knowledgeable enough to separate the wheat from the chaff. Even the magazines which cater to the archer sometimes accept material which raises eyebrows among veteran bow hunters.

Here, for example, are quotes from an article presumably written by a bow hunter of some note who was testing a compound bow in the field. He admits in print, "It came back all right, about four or five inches, but with might and main, I couldn't break over the eccentric cams to the relaxed position."

Obviously, this writer had not tested the bow on the target line before taking it to the hunting scene. It would certainly appear that his first attempt was on a living animal. Otherwise he would have known his physical limitation and would have made proper adjustments.

"I tried again to pull my arrow to full draw. No way!"

No way, indeed.

Another writer admitted that Blank of Blank Archery Company, ". . . had given me this bow to field-test only twenty-four hours before the hunt."

No thinking hunter has much regard for the fellow who takes a strange rifle into the field without first test-firing it. It is close to criminal to go hunting with a bow that has not been tested with specific arrows for the purpose of hunting big game.

We are not hunting targets. We are seeking to take a living creature that certainly deserves the best we can deliver.

If *this* writer appears to take himself too seriously, he makes no apologies for it. There are no excuses to offer; only the attempt to substantiate opinions proffered.

This book is loaded with expressions such as *perhaps, probably, may, sometimes, usually.* There is no literary shrinking behind the employment of such escapisms. Those who have traveled the same trails will recognize that in the human association with Nature there are no positives.

Anyone who professes to know what any wild creature will do under every situation is a fool. We hunt under the laws of probability with anticipation of uncertainty and the strong possibility that we may blow the whole deal.

It's rather like writing a book.

Glossary

Archery has a language of its own, and some terms will probably be less familiar to readers than others. Many have come down through the ages; some have been coined to describe new developments. What follows is enough to acquaint even the newcomer with the common and not-so-common words that belong to the sport. Some hunting terms have slightly different meanings in various parts of the country and are identified according to their use in this book.

Anchor: where archer's drawing hand is positioned at full draw.

Archer:
> Bare bow—contestant or hunter who shoots with no aiming device on bow.
>
> Bow hunter—generally one who counts hunting as the principal archery pastime; a bow hunter's tournament class is recognized as the heavy tackle division.
>
> Target—contestant who utilizes sights and any other shooting assists permitted in a specific contest.

Arrow:
> Crest—identifying stripes or pattern on the shaft forward of fletching.
>
> Fletching—feather or plastic vanes to guide shaft.
>
> Head—*target*, generally light with modified taper.
>> *blunt*, flattened for random target practice and small game.
>>
>> *broadhead*, usually ⅞" or more in width with two or more cutting blades, for big game.
>>
>> *field*, pointed, for field target shooting and small game and may be matched in weight with broadhead.
>>
>> *fish*, barbed to insure sticking, generally with hole drilled in base for attaching line.

Nock—plastic fitting to set arrow on bow string, at one time cut into rear of shaft or made separate of harder wood.

Rest—shelf or attachment where arrow is positioned on bow.

Shaft—generally the bare length without component parts; sometimes substituted for the word *arrow* itself.

Arm guard: bracer, protecting strip or partial sheath which is attached to forearm to avoid string slap or interference.

Bow:

Back—surface away from bow at the ready.

Belly, or face—surface of bow facing archer at the ready.

Compound—basic flat bow to which an arrangement of pulleys, eccentric wheels and cables have been added to increase performance.

Grip—handle (terms are interchangeable).

Hunting—usually shorter, frequently camouflaged, heavy weight bow for big game also used sometimes in field competition.

Limb—working extension of bow from handle or riser section.

Nock—notched end of limb to accommodate string.

Recurve—as distinguished from straight longbow, generally of laminations of fiberglass and wood, with tips of limbs curving away from archer.

Riser (section)—stationary handle section from which limbs extend or to which they are fastened.

Self—made of one piece of one material, generally wood; seldom seen any more.

Shelf—arrow rest.

Takedown—also called *take apart, collapsible, jointed,* etc., in either target or hunting weight, which comes in two or three parts which join together.

Target—one used generally for target shooting, interchangeable as hunting bow in heavier weights.

Weight—energy needed to draw an arrow 28 inches according to archery manufacturers organization specifications.

Window—cut-away area, riser, of handle area on modern bows which permits arrow to rest at longitudinal center of bow.

Bowstringer: device used to string bows so that side stress or limb twisting can be avoided.

Brace: to string a bow.

Cast: the capacity of a bow to utilize its maximum power potential in driving an arrow.

Creeping: tendency of an archer to permit string to relax somewhat after reaching full draw.

Crossbow: a bow mounted on a stock which is activated by a trigger.

Draw: to pull the string on a bow; that position when a given archer has pulled the string so that he reaches his maximum potential as the full arrow shaft is utilized and his drawing hand is anchored in position.

Hunting:

Drive—cooperative effort of more than one hunter to move game toward waiting hunter or hunters or toward each other.

Stalk—attempt to move close enough to shoot at a selected game animal.

Stand—a stationary position likely to produce shooting.

Still—waiting for game to approach a blind or stand.

Watch—interchangeable with still hunting. (Depending on geographical area, the terms standers, watchers and sitters might be considered synonymous.)

Jumping the string: ability of animal to move at sight and/or sound of bow shot in time to avoid arrow.

Pod: rubber sleeve, containing poisonous amount of tranquilizing drug to kill big game, which fits behind broadhead so that substance can enter blood stream.

Quiver:

Back—traditional arrow receptacle fastened by one strap over shoulder (other variations).

Belt—arrow receptacle which fastens to waist belt common in target archery.

Bow—arrow receptacle which screws to or is clipped to riser section.

Reel (bow):   stationary spool onto which heavy line is attached from fish arrow so that aquatic game can be recovered.

Shooting: releasing the arrow, loosing.

Sight (bow):   aiming device adapted for use with bow and arrow.

Spine: amount of stiffness in an arrow shaft.

Stabilizer: an extended weighted rod or knob to add mass weight and to dampen instability of bow and bow arm, seldom used on hunting bows.

String:

Brush button—device attached near bow tip to avoid catching brush.

Height—distance of string from throat of grip; fistmele; brace height.

Loop—braided and served eye in each end which fastens to bow nock.

Nocking point—addition of material to serving to mark exact point at which arrow should be nocked each time.

Serving—wrapping of similar material to resist friction of arrow release and to protect any area which comes in contact with bow itself.

Appendix

Although it is certain that some laws and regulations will change from time to time, what follows should be a base of information for many years to come. It was obtained through a questionnaire sent to each of the United States and the Canadian provinces.

It should benefit the bow hunter who may not be completely familiar with the rules in his resident hunting area. But, it is primarily for those who plan to hunt in other areas. Of course, there are states and provinces which combine bow hunting with gun hunting. The approximate dates for each species are times when bow hunting is legal, whether or not it is a gunning season.

Since there is always a possibility of error as well as likely changes, each archer has a responsibility to check carefully before hunting in another state or province. This is a guide, not a legal presentation. At the beginning of each subdivision is the proper address for obtaining current information.

THE UNITED STATES
ALABAMA

Department of Conservation, Division of Game & Fish, Montgomery, Alabama 36104

License: Resident state

L & S game	$ 5.25
county	
L & S game	2.75
Nonresident	
Small game	10.50
7-Day	7.15
All game (inc.	
deer & turkeys)	25.15
7-Day All game	10.15

Bow Hunting: No special tag—regular license. No special tackle requirements. No crossbows; no poison heads. Compound bow under consideration. Both residents and nonresidents pay $3.15 for special tag for hunting on State Game Management Areas.

Use of dogs permitted in certain counties; all small game in regular season with bow; fox, bobcat, beaver, nutria during daylight hours throughout the year; bucks only in certain counties; antlerless deer, certain counties; spring turkey gobbler season bows only in certain counties. Antlered deer limit—one a day.

Seasons

Deer—Oct. 10 to Jan. 24, outside dates. First month archery only in many counties. Antlered or antlerless (one a season) deer designated by counties. Bow only in certain counties for spring turkey season (5 bird limit for season).
Number of bow hunters (est.) 12,000.

ALASKA

Alaska Department of Fish & Game, Subport Bldg., Juneau, Alaska 99801

License:

Resident	$ 10.00
Nonresident	20.00
Tag fees for:	
Bison	100.00
Deer	25.00
Black bear	75.00
Brown bear	150.00
Grizzly bear	150.00
Elk	75.00
Moose	100.00
Caribou	50.00
Sheep	150.00
Mt. goats	75.00
Wolf	50.00
Wolverine	25.00
Musk oxen	1,000.00

Bow Hunting: No special tag—regular license. Barbed arrows outlawed. Crossbows, compound bows and poison heads permitted (except for brown and grizzly bears in Units 1 through 5 in Southeast). No minimum requirements on bows and arrows. A licensed guide is required for hunting sheep, brown and grizzly bears. No bears with cubs may be shot.

Use of dogs only on black bears and then by permit. Arctic hare, snowshoe hare, ptarmigan, spruce, sharp-tailed and ruffed grouse, and waterfowl in season. Also, foxes, coyotes, lynx, porcupines permitted.

Seasons

Bison—limited permit hunt in Sept.; Musk oxen, Nunivak Island, bulls only by special periods; Deer, generally Aug. 1, to Dec. 31, with cut-off dates for antlerless deer; Black bears, some areas no closed season, others generally early Aug. or Sept. 1 to following June 30; Brown and grizzly bears seasons roughly mid-Oct. to end Nov. or Dec. with spring seasons in May to June; Elk, Aug. 1 to Dec. 31; Moose, earliest Aug. 1 through Dec. 31 with many local variations; Caribou, from no closed seasons to no open season, but usually in protected areas from Aug. 10 through Mar. 31; Sheep, about Aug. 10 to Sept. 20; Goats, outside dates, Aug. 1 to Jan. 31, but many variations; Wolf, where there are seasons, Sept. 1 through April 30; Wolverines, generally Sept. 1 to March 31; Foxes and lynx generally follow wolf seasons.

Number of bow hunters unknown.

ARIZONA

Arizona Game & Fish Department, 2222 W. Greenway Road, Phoenix, Arizona 85023

License:	Resident	$ 7.00	Bow Hunting: No special tag. Special
	Nonresident	30.00	archery seasons on deer, elk and javelinas.
	Tag fees for:		Bow must be 40 lbs. Arrowheads
	Deer	30.00	minimum width ⅞". Crossbows and
	Elk	75.00	poison arrows not permitted. Compound
	Javelinas	20.00	bow is legal. On Indian reservations,
	Antelope	50.00	tribal permits are required.
	Black bear	25.00	
	Big horn sheep	250.00	
	Lion	10.00	
	Turkeys	10.00	

Use of dogs on bears and lions permitted. All small game in season and all predators may be taken except porcupines, ocelots, jaguars and wolves. Application for special fee tags are available by July 17, for big game except javelinas and turkeys which are available by Dec. 18.

Seasons

Special archery seasons for: deer, Sept. 8 to 24 in certain areas, Dec. 1 to 31 in others, and Navajo Indian Reservation Oct. 7 to 22. Any deer legal; javelina, Jan. 20 to Feb. 12, in specified areas; elk, Sept. 8 to 22 by limited number of permits over large area of state, any elk: turkeys, Sept. 8 to 24 in designated areas, any turkey.

Number of bow hunters (est.), 4,500.

ARKANSAS

Arkansas Game & Fish Commission, Little Rock, Arkansas 72201

License: Resident $ 3.50   Bow Hunting: Bow hunting tag may
Nonresident 30.00   be bought just for this purpose. Bow
Archery only   minimum weight 40 lbs. at 28" draw.
(1 deer, 1   Arrowheads must have minimum of ⅛"
turkey) 10.00   cutting surface. Crossbows are permitted
during firearms season only. Compound
bows legal. No answer on poison heads.

No answer on use of dogs. Squirrels and rabbits may be taken on archery tag. Coyotes and bobcats also legal quarry.

Seasons

Deer—months of Oct. through Jan. Turkeys usually in months of October and April.
Number of bow hunters (est.), 15,000.

CALIFORNIA

Department of Fish & Game, 1416 Ninth Street, Sacramento, California 95814

License: Resident $ 6.00   Bow Hunting: No special tag—regular
Nonresident 35.00   license. Bow must be capable of casting
Tag fees for: hunting arrow 130 yards; arrowhead
Deer 25.00   must have cutting edge no less than ⅛".
Black bear 1.00   Compound bows are legal; poison heads
and crossbows are not legal for hunting.

Use of dogs not permitted in special archery seasons. Permitted (one dog) in firearms seasons for deer, and (3 dogs) for pigs. License permits taking, during large game season, mountain quail, Sierra grouse, raccoons and opossums. Coyotes, bobcats and skunks may also be shot. Archer may hunt in regular gunning season on tag. Bears may not be baited nor may they be shot within a 400-yard radius of a garbage dump. Pigs are legal over state year-around except Monterey County.

Seasons

Two deer seasons for archers are held. First, about July 8 to 23; second, about Aug. 19 to Sept. 12. A special bow season for turkeys is held about the third week in Nov. of 9 days. Bears may be taken with the bow from about Aug. 19 to Sept. 12, except in the areas of the early deer season, and may be taken in the regular bear season in certain areas, Oct. to Jan. 1.
Number of bow hunters (est.), 35,000.

COLORADO

Division of Wildlife, Dept. of Natural Resources, 6060 Broadway, Denver,
    Colorado 80216

License:	Resident	Game	Nonresident
	$10.00	Antelope	$25.00
	7.50	Deer	25.00
	*5.00	Black bear	25.00
	10.00	Elk	25.00
	*40.00	Sheep	(not eligible)
	* 5.00	Turkey	*10.00

Bow Hunting: No small game or vermin permitted without a regular small-game license. Regular big-game license (deer or elk) required to use bow in firearm season. Compound bow permitted; no crossbow nor poison heads allowed. Bow must be capable of casting arrow 130 yards. Mechanical release for arrow *or string* outlawed.

*Regular firearm license permits taking of these species with bow; all others require special tag as noted.

Dogs permitted during bear or lion season that does not run concurrent with deer, elk, antelope or sheep.

Seasons

Antelope—early Nov. to end of month. Deer—mid-Aug. to mid-Sept. Black bears —no special bow season; may be hunted during regular seasons. Elk—same as deer in specific areas. Sheep—mid-August to early Sept. (1972 first bow season in one specific area only) Turkeys—regular firearm season only, but bow permitted. Number of bow hunters—11,860.

CONNECTICUT

State Board of Fisheries and Game, State Office Bldg., Hartford, Connecticut 06115

License:	Resident	$ 4.35
	Nonresident	13.35
	Tag fee for	
	deer	5.25
	(all hunters)	

Bow Hunting: Small game and foxes may be taken in season, most are legal. Written permission to hunt must be obtained from landowner on private property. Bow must be capable of casting 400 grain arrow 150 yards. Arrow must carry full name and address of owner. Head of two blades or more of not less than ⅞″ cutting width; not permitted—crossbow, compound bow, poison heads. Hunter must be 16 years of age. List of state-owned lands available with license.

Seasons

Deer—Nov. 1 through Dec. 31. One deer of either sex.
    Number of bow hunters—3,654.

DELAWARE

Dept. of Natural Resources & Environmental Control, Division of Fish & Wildlife, D Street, Dover Delaware 19901

License: Resident $ 5.20
        Nonresident 25.25

Bow Hunting: No special tag needed. Any small game in season may be taken. No minimums on tackle except that broadhead must be sharpened and of no less than ⅞" in width. No crossbows, compound bows or poison arrows are permitted.

Seasons

Deer: Sept. 1 through Oct. 31; Jan. 1 through Jan. 13.
    Number of bow hunters (mail survey), 1,900.

FLORIDA

Game & Fresh Water Fish Commission, Bryant Bldg., Tallahasse, Florida 32304

License: Resident
      State $ 7.50
      Home county 2.00
      Other counties 4.50
      Archery permit 5.00
    Nonresident
      State 26.50
      State—10 day 11.50
      Archery permit 5.00

Bow Hunting: No dogs; no crossbows; no poison arrows. Compound bow okay. All legal game except turkeys and wild hogs in most areas. Bow must be capable of casting one ounce arrow 150 yards. No tree stands over 8 ft.

Seasons

Deer (except fawn) certain counties—about Sept. 9 through Sept. 29. Special hunts. Two deer season limit. Bears—In Baker or Columbia Counties. Turkey, quail, rabbits, squirrel, wild hogs and unprotected fur-bearing animals in deer season (fox, raccoon, opossum, etc.).
    Number of bow hunters (1972), 9,740.

GEORGIA

Dept. of Natural Resources, Trinity-Washington Street S. W., Atlanta, Georgia
    30334

License: Resident $ 4.25   Bow Hunting: No special tags. Any small
          Nonresident   25.25   game may be taken in season. Also, fox,
          10-day   15.25   coyote, armadilla and bobcat. May hunt
          Resident bow   in gunning season with archery tag. Bow
            and arrow   3.25   minimum weight is 40 lbs. Minimum
          Nonresident   broadhead ⅞" in width. Crossbows,
            bow & arrow   compound bows and poison arrows
            season   25.25   illegal.
          10-day   12.50

Seasons

Deer: October plus special management areas. Turkeys: regular spring season in
April.
      Number of bow hunters—22,152.

HAWAII

Division of Fish & Game, 1179 Punchbowl St., Honolulu, Hawaii 96813

License: Resident $ 7.50   Bow Hunting: No special tag; regular
          Nonresident   15.00   on all islands. Bow weight minimum of
                                            45 lbs. for long bows, 35 lbs. for
                                            full-recurve bows. No poison arrows,
                                            crossbows; compound bows legal.
                                            Broadhead points only. Tags required
                                            for feral sheep only. Special archery
                                            areas. Permits and reporting required in
                                            certain areas. Limited use of dogs. Small
                                            game permitted in season.

Seasons

Feral pigs—some areas year-around. Feral goats follow pig season. Feral sheep in
August and September in certain areas; year-around in others. Some areas open
only on weekends and holidays. Antelope—August. Deer—March & April. Turkeys—November.
      Number of bow hunters unknown.

IDAHO

Idaho Fish & Game Dept., 600 S. Walnut, P. O. Box 25, Boise, Idaho 83707

License: Resident

	Fish & Game	$ 6.00
	Game only	3.00
	Antelope	8.00
	Elk tag	3.00
	Bears	2.00
	Deer tag	2.00
	Moose	35.00
	Sheep	35.00
	Goats	15.00
	Turkey	5.00
Nonresident		
	Fish & Game	135.00
	Deer only	75.00
	(plus tag)	2.00
	Bear only	25.00
	(plus tag)	2.00
	Cougar tag	10.00
	Antelope tag	8.00
	Elk tag	3.00
	Moose tag	35.00
	Sheep tag	35.00
	Goat tag	15.00
	Turkey tag	5.00

Bow Hunting: No special archery tag. But, full fish & game license needed for all species except special deer and bear licenses (plus tags). Bow weight 40 lb., minimum at 28" draw; ⅞" broadhead. No poison arrows; no crossbows in special archery seasons. Compound bow permitted. Rabbits, forest grouse, quail and partridge in season. Controlled hunts by permit. Antlered deer only on special deer license.

(Extra deer tag with nonresident fish & game license)

Deer—seasons by areas with dates from early Sept. to mid-Dec. Antelope—early Aug. to mid-Sept. by area. Elk—early Sept. to late Dec. by area. Bears—generally most of Sept., local exceptions. Goats—most of Sept. by area. Other animals in regular firearms season.

Number of bow hunters unknown.

ILLINOIS

Department of Conservation, 605 State Office Bldg., Springfield, Illinois 62700

License:	Resident	$5.00
	Bow tag	5.00
	No nonresident	
	big-game license.	

Bow Hunting—For residents only. May shoot any small game in season. Same for vermin. Minimum bow weight, 40 lbs. No crossbows or poison arrows. Compound bow permitted.

Seasons

Deer—Oct. 1 through Dec. 31, except closed during gunning season.

Number of bow hunters—14,841.

INDIANA

Dept. of Natural Resources, State Office Bldg., Room 607, Indianapolis, Indiana 46204

License:	Resident	$ 5.75	Bow Hunting—No small game or vermin
	Turkey		may be shot in big-game season with bow
	Nonresident	5.25	on big-game license. Minimum bow
	Deer	25.75	weight 35 lbs. Metal edged broadhead
	Turkey	15.75	only. No crossbows. Compound bow
			legal.

Seasons

Deer—Archery season, either sex, about Oct. 13 through Nov. 10. Bucks only, about Dec. 3 through Dec. 12. Turkeys, regular season only, about April 25 through 29.

Number of bow hunters—18,504 (including 97 nonresidents).

IOWA

Iowa Conservation Commission, 300 Fourth Street, Des Moines, Iowa 50319

License:	Resident	$ 5.00	Bow Hunting—For residents only.
	Deer Tag	10.00	Crossbow prohibited; no poison arrows.
	No nonresident		Compound bow permitted. Broadhead
	big-game license.		points only.

Season

Deer—About Oct. 7 through Nov. 26, any deer.
Number of bow hunters—7,359.

KANSAS

Forestry, Fish & Game Commission, Box 1028, Pratt, Kansas 67124

License:	Resident	$ 3.00	Bow Hunting—Only one permit, archery
	(increases		or firearms, issued to resident. Minimum
	anticipated)		bow weight 35 lbs. No crossbows or
	Antelope tag	10.00	poison arrows. Compound bow permitted.
	Deer tag	10.00	Steel broadhead only.
	Turkey tag	10.00	
	No nonresident		
	big-game license		

Seasons

Deer—Oct. 1 through Nov. 30.
Number of bow hunters—4,123.

KENTUCKY

Dept. of Fish & Wildlife Resources, Frankfort, Kentucky 40601

License: Resident $ 5.00
        Deer tag 10.50
        Nonresident 27.50
        (Deer permit required on
        "Land Between the Lakes")

Bow Hunting: Any small game in season except migratory birds. Also, gray fox. No dogs for deer. Long bows only except crossbows of 80-lb. pull permitted in Pioneer Weapons Area. Arrowheads must be barbless and ⅞" min. width. Any deer. No dogs for deer.

Seasons

Deer—Archery, generally months of Oct. and Dec. Regular turkey, May spring season; fall, late Oct. Land Between Lakes Area, archery, last two weeks of Dec.
    Number of bow hunters (last survey in 1970), 11,700.

LOUISIANA

Louisiana Wild Life & Fisheries Commission, P. O. Box 44095, Capitol Station, Baton Rouge, Louisiana 70804

License: Resident $ 2.00
        Deer & turkey tag 2.00
        Nonresident 25.00
        2-day trip 5.00
        Plus big-game tag 2.00

Bow Hunting: Rabbits, squirrels, turkeys and quail legal in big-game season. Also foxes, wildcats, coyote and armadillo. No special archery tag. Bow minimum weight 30 lbs. Metal broadhead ⅞" minimum width. Crossbows legal for amputees only. Compound bows illegal. No poison arrows. Dogs legal in some areas for deer. Archery deer, still hunting only, any deer. Orange cloth (400 sq. inches) on head, front or back. One deer a day; five the season.

Seasons

Deer—archery season, Oct. through mid-Jan. Hogs legal in some areas. Check local regulations for big game.
    Number of bow hunters—from computer estimate (1971–72)—12,000.

MAINE

Commissioner of Inland Fisheries & Game, State House, Augusta, Maine 04330

License: Resident $ 6.50
        Bow license 6.50
        Nonresident 42.50

Bow Hunting: All small game in season and vermin legal. One license good for all seasons. Bow must be able to cast arrow 150 yards. Broadhead ⅞" minimum width. No crossbows or poison arrows. Compound bow legal. One deer for season. Bow legal in regular fall gunning season and spring bear season.

Seasons

Deer and black bears—October.
Number of bow hunters—1,164.

MARYLAND

Dept. of Natural Resources, Wildlife Administration, Natural Resources Bldg.,
Annapolis, Maryland 21401

License:	Resident	$ 6.50	Bow Hunting: Bow not less than 30 lbs.;
	Deer & turkey		broadhead, minimum metal not less than
	stamp	5.50	7⁄8″. No crossbows nor poison arrows.
	*Nonresident	25.00	Compound bow okay. No dogs. Any deer
	Deer & archery		in archery season. Small game in season.
	stamp	5.50	Same for vermin (fox is protected in
	*(reciprocity—		some counties).
	same as state of		
	origin but not less		
	than listed)		

Seasons

Deer—Sept. 15 through Nov. 24; Dec. 3 through Jan. 1. Firearms and bow
(bucks only) Nov. 25 through Dec. 2 (except antlerless deer by county permit).
Turkeys—In season fall and spring. Foxes—protected in some parts of Maryland.
Number of bow hunters (1972) est., 5,000.

MASSACHUSETTS

Division of Fisheries & Game, 100 Cambridge St., Government Center, Boston,
Massachusetts 02202

License:	Resident	$ 8.25	Bow Hunting: Bow may be used during
	Archery stamp	5.10	three-weeks' archery season and one-week
	Bear stamp	.50	firearm season. Any deer in archery
	Nonresident	35.25	season. Minimum bow weight 40 lbs;
	Archery stamp	5.10	7⁄8″ minimum broadhead width. Arrow
	Bear stamp	.50	shaft must be marked with owner's
			name and address. No crossbows or
			poison arrows. Compound bow permitted.

Seasons

Deer—Archery, about Nov. 5 through Nov. 24; firearms (and bow) first week of
Dec. Black bears—about Nov. 19 through Nov. 24.
Number of bow hunters (estimated), 5,200.

MICHIGAN

Department of Natural Resources, Lansing, Michigan 48926

License: Resident Archery
    Deer & bears $ 7.50
    Sportsman (all
      fish and game) 18.50
  Nonresident
  archery
    Deer & bears   20.00
  Special archery
    bear tag for mid-
    Sept. through
    Oct. 31   5.00

Bow Hunting—No small game without regular small-game license ($25.00). Same for vermin. No minimum on bows and arrows except, no crossbows or poison arrows. Compound bow legal if locked in car trunk or rendered incapable of being shot when not in use. All bows must be unstrung when in motor vehicle, aircraft, ATV, motorboat, sailboat, trail bike or snowmobile. Archer can't hunt in gunning deer season without regular license. No dogs.

Seasons

Deer—Oct. 1 through Dec. 31, except Nov. 15 through Nov. 30. Black bears—Oct. 1 through Nov. 14. Turkeys—Small-game license required in spring season (May).

Number of bow hunters, 68,250 (1971). More under Sportsman license.

MINNESOTA

Dept. of Natural Resources, Centennial Office Bldg., Saint Paul, Minnesota 55155

License: Resident $ 7.50
  Nonresident   10.25
  (Both R. and N.
  good for bow
  and arrow only
  for bears and deer
  during archery and
  firearms regular
  seasons)
  Bear tag   5.00
  (for special Sept.-
  Oct. season)

Bow Hunting—All licenses must be purchased before or on Nov. 1. Bow minimum 40 lbs. Minimum width 1″ for arrowheads of not less than 110 grains if all steel; 90 grains if plastic core or ferrule. Special areas for hunting. No bears to be shot within ¼ mi. of dump or in den. No cub bears. No crossbows; no poison arrows. Compound bow okay. No small game without license. All vermin—fox, coyote, badger, wolf, raccoon, etc.—permitted on archery license. Hours—sunrise to sunset. No dogs.

Seasons

Deer—usually Oct. and Nov. Early Dec. in southeast section of state. Bears—mid-Sept. to about Oct. 21. Moose—special seasons by legislation and drawing—residents only.

Number of bow hunters—20,000.

MISSISSIPPI

Mississippi Game & Fish Commission, Box 451, Jackson, Mississippi 39205

License: Residents $ 5.00   Bow Hunting: Small game in season okay
        Deer & turkey tag   2.00   on archery license. Also vermin, fox &
        Extra deer tag   5.00   bobcat. May hunt in firearms season
        Archery license   with proper license. Crossbows illegal;
          for special season   3.00   compound bows okay. No ruling on
        Nonresident   poison arrows. No dogs in archery
          (all game)   25.00   seasons.
        7-day all game   10.00
        Deer & turkey tag   2.00
        Extra deer tag   5.00
        Special deer only
          archery season   5.00
        Additional fee
          to establish
          reciprocity in
          state of
          residence, but
          not less than
          above.

Seasons

Deer—generally month of Oct. and first two weeks of Nov. (firearms seasons in late Nov., again in Dec. into Jan.). Primitive weapons third week of Dec. Extra deer buck tag good in other than archery seasons. Turkeys—gobbler season, bows only, last week of April.

Number of bow hunters—9,566.

MISSOURI

Dept. of Conservation, North Ten Mile Drive, Jefferson City, Missouri 65101

License: Resident Firearms $ 7.80   Bow Hunting—All small game in season
        Archery Deer   7.80   and vermin may be taken on nonresident
        Turkey   7.80   license. Hours—5:30 a.m. to 6:00 p.m.
        Nonresident   up to Nov. 17; 6:30 a.m. to 5:00 p.m.
        archery   15.30   thereafter. Any deer. Bow legal in
        Firearms   30.30   firearms season with proper license. No
        Turkeys   30.30   minimums on bows or arrows. Crossbow
           illegal on archery license; no poison
           arrows. Compound bow legal. No dogs.

Seasons

Deer—Oct., Nov. & Dec. special archery season. May take second deer on firearms license with bow or gun.

Number of bow hunters—17,840.

MONTANA

Dept. of Fish & Game, Helena, Montana, 59601

License:

Resident		
sportsman	$ 20.25	
fishing & hunting		
plus one each,		
black bear, deer,		
elk.		
Pre-gun archery	3.00	
Antelope tag	3.00	
Moose tag	25.00	
Goat tag	15.00	
Sheep tag	25.00	
Grizzly bear tag	25.00	
Turkeys	2.00	
Nonresident	151.00	
all regular hunting		
and fishing plus		
1 elk, 2 deer		
Black bear		
spring license	35.00	
Special deer &		
antelope	35.00	
Black bear tag	35.00	
Grizzly bear kill tag	25.00	

With $151.00 combination license on drawing under quotas.

Antelope tag	$ 10.00
Moose tag	50.00
Goat tag	30.00
Sheep tag	50.00
Pre-gun archery	3.00

plus specific game tag.

Turkey license	25.00

Bow Hunting: Wide open spaces may make bow hunting practical in firearms season. Crossbow illegal in special archery season. Poison arrows illegal. Compound bow okay. Guides at $50 and up per day required (outfitters), or resident guide required on Nat'l Forest, Wilderness Area, Nat'l Game Refuge or State Game Range. Landowner may guide or permit nonguided hunting on fenced land. Commission may designate nonguide deer and antelope areas. All small game and vermin legal in archery season. No minimum on bow weights or arrows. Tags extra after purchase of regular license. Grizzly bear kill tag on top of regular license and special grizzly hunting tag.

Seasons

Antelope, elk and deer—generally mid-Sept. to mid-Oct. for special archery season. All others—generally mid-Oct. to late Nov. Spring black bear season.

Number of bow hunters—6,200.

NEBRASKA

Nebraska Game & Parks Commission, Box 65, Bassett, Nebraska 68714

License: Resident
    Archery deer
      permit $10.00
    Archery antelope
      permit   10.00
    Nonresident
    Archery
      deer permit   30.00
    Archery antelope
      permit   30.00

Bow Hunting: No small game or vermin legal on big-game permit. No hunting in gunning season without firearms permit ($30.00). Bow weight minimum 40 lbs. at 28" draw. Broadhead blades 7/16" radius, no crossbows nor poison arrows. Compound bow okay. No restriction on use of dogs.

Seasons

Deer (archery) about last week of Sept. through Nov. 9; Nov. 20 through end of year. Antelope (archery) about Aug. 19 through Sept. 22; month of October.
    Number of bow hunters: Deer, 5980; Antelope, 122—Total 6,012.

NEVADA

Nevada Dept. of Fish & Game, P.O. Box 10678, Reno, Nevada 89510

License: Resident $ 5.00
    Deer tags:
      Regular   5.00
    Post-season   5.00
    Post-season
      anterless   5.00
    Archery   5.00
    Nonresident
      regular   30.00
    Archery
      license   10.00
    Archery
      hunting tag   30.00

Bow Hunting: Regulations confusing. Questionnaire had scanty answers. Bow must be capable of casting 400-grain arrow 150 yards. Arrow must have 3/4-inch wide hunting-type tip. Crossbow illegal. Compound okay. Licenses issued by quota for specified areas. Foxes may be taken on archery tag. No answer on poison arrows. Dogs legal only for lions. Changes in regulations anticipated.

Seasons

Archery: Deer—About last week of Aug. through most of Sept. Antelope—Residents only.
    Number of bow hunters—estimated—1,200.

NEW HAMPSHIRE

Dept. of Fish & Game, Concord, New Hampshire, 03301

License: Resident Archery $ 4.25

Nonresident Regular 15.50

Nonresident 40.50

Bow hunter needs only archery license 15.50

Bow Hunting: No dogs for deer—okay for bear; not more than six in group hunt; no artificial noise-makers for driving; no crossbows; no poison arrows. Compound bow okay. Small game—rabbits, grouse, pheasant, and raccoons may be taken in season. Also vermin—foxes, coyotes, porcupines. Archer may hunt in gun season. Minimum bow weight 40 lbs.; broad head minimum ⅞" width; maximum 1-½"; name and address of user must be affixed.

Seasons

Deer—Oct. 1 to end of season each year. (Gun season Nov. 10 through first Sunday in Dec.) Black bear—Sept. 1 to end of deer season. Wild hogs—No closed season.

Number of bow hunters—nonresident 518; resident 1,408; total 1,926.

NEW JERSEY

Department of Environmental Protection, Division of Fish, Game & Shell Fisheries, P. O. Box 1809, Trenton, New Jersey 08625

License: Resident firearms $ 7.25

Resident archery 7.25

Nonresident firearms 25.25

Nonresident archery 25.25

(both *not* required)

Bow Hunting: No small game in big-game season; foxes legal. Small game in season. Minimum bow weight 35 lbs.; broadhead minimum width ¾"—maximum width1-½"; length 1-½". Bow must cast arrow 125 yards. No crossbows, poison arrows. Compound bow legal. Bow must be wrapped, cased or carried in trunk of car during hours of darkness.

Seasons

Deer—About Oct. 7 through Nov. 9, either sex; about Dec. 4 through Dec. 9, bucks only.

Number of bow hunters—30,680.

NEW MEXICO

Dept. of Game & Fish, State Capitol, Sante Fe, New Mexico 87501

License:	Resident:		Nonresident:
Regular big game (good for deer, bears, turkeys, squirrels)		$ 7.50	$ 50.25
Deer (bow hunting) (any deer license)			15.00
General big game & birds		9.00	Not issued
General hunting & fishing		12.00	Not issued
Additional deer in 2-deer areas		3.00	6.00
Special season deer tag		2.00	2.00
Bears—before & after deer season		Not issued	25.00
Bird		5.00	17.00
Antelope		10.00	40.00
Elk		15.00	50.00
Barbary sheep		20.00	100.00
Bighorn sheep		20.00	100.00
Cougar		10.00	100.00
Non-game animals		Not required	10.00 (or any non-resident license)

Bow Hunting: Dogs legal at times on bear, cougar, grouse and squirrel. Elk, antelope and sheep licenses available only by application. Bows must be capable of casting a hunting arrow at least 130 yards. Broadheads with steel cutting edges. Small game legal in season. Also other non-game species. No crossbows nor poison arrows. Compound bow legal. Tribal permits needed on Indian lands. Permits needed on private lands.

Seasons

Deer—Generally mid-Oct. to as late as end of Jan., depending on area. Either sex. Sandia Mountain special. Antelope—Special bow hunts in late Aug. and late Sept. Either sex. Varied season on above and other game too extensive to cover here. Get annual "Hunting Proclamation".

Number of bow hunters—6,541.

NEW YORK

New York Conservation Dept., Albany, New York 12201

License: Resident $ 4.25
          Archery tag   3.25
          Big game   4.25
          Nonresident   35.00
          Archery tag   3.25

Bow Hunting: All small game may be taken in season—rabbits, grouse, squirrels, varying hare, raccoons, and all unprotected wildlife. May hunt in gunning seasons. No minimum bow; broadheads must have two or more cutting edges with minimum width ⅞". No crossbows nor poison arrows; compound bow legal. Bow only in Westchester County. Must show license to *anybody* on request. Sunday hunting with bow. Any deer. Holders of party permit may take one extra deer in area specified. No dogs.

Seasons

Deer—Northern zone, 14 days, immediately preceding firearms season which opens generally about Oct. 25. Southern zone, 16 days, immediately preceding firearms season which opens generally about Nov. 20. Bear—Coincides with deer bow hunting seasons.

Number of bow hunters—57,629.

NORTH CAROLINA

Wildlife Resources Commission, Rawleigh, North Carolina 27602

License: Resident $ 5.50
          Big game tag   1.75
          Nonresident   22.00
          Big game tag   1.75
          Six-day license   17.75

Bow Hunting: Since no special archery license, all game and legal non-game animals and birds may be taken with bow. Antlerless deer only in areas where gunners may also take antlerless deer. Bows not less than 45 pounds. Broadhead non-barbed with minimum ⅞" width. Blunts okay for small game and birds. No crossbows nor poison arrows; compound bow okay. No bears with cubs. One bear, one deer a day. Two deer per season.

Seasons

Deer—Where firearms season opens Nov. 20, special bow season Oct. 20 through Nov. 11; where firearms season opens Oct. 16, bow season Sept. 22 through Oct. 14. Bears—Mid-Oct. to mid-Nov. Mid-Dec. to Jan. 1. Wild boar—Same as bear seasons. Turkeys—About April 21 through May 12.

Number of bow hunters (estimated), 10,000.

NORTH DAKOTA

Game & Fish Dept., Bismark, North Dakota 58501

License:	Resident	$ 7.00
	Nonresident	25.00

Bow Hunting—May take rabbits. Small-game tag needed for other species. May not use bow in gun season without firearms license. No age limits for bow hunter. Bow must be capable of casting arrow 130 yards. Minimum arrow length 24", broadhead minimums—width ¾"; length 1-½". No crossbows nor poison arrows. Compound bow okay. No hunting before noon on opening days. One deer, any sex. No dogs.

Seasons

Deer—Aug. 25 through Nov. 5; Nov. 20 through Dec. 31. Antelope—Aug. 25 through Sept. 17; Oct. 2 through Nov. 5. Turkeys—residents only.
   Number of bow hunters—Resident 4,558; Nonresident 121; total 4,679.

OHIO

Ohio Dept. of Natural Resources, Division of Wildlife, 1500 Dublin Road, Columbus, Ohio 43215

License:	Resident	$ 4.35
	Deer permit	5.35
	Turkey permit	5.35
	Nonresident	20.25
	Deer permit	5.35
	Turkey permit	5.35

Bow Hunting: No minimums on bow or arrows. No crossbows nor poison arrows. Compound bow okay. All small game in season; no vermin legal. Any deer. One a season. May hunt in firearms season. No dogs.

Seasons

Deer—About Oct. 13 through Jan. 6. Short firearms season in late Nov., early Dec., by counties. Turkeys—First two weeks in May by counties—bearded birds only.
   Number of bow hunters—10,000.

OKLAHOMA

Dept. of Wildlife Conservation, 1801 N. Lincoln, P. O. Box 53465, Oklahoma City, Oklahoma 73105

License:	Resident	$ 3.25
	Deer tag	5.00
	Turkey tag	3.00
	Regular	
	Nonresident	15.00
	Deer tag	25.00
	Turkey tag	15.00

Bow Hunting: Entire state open to bow hunting with local exceptions. Small game in season. Also foxes and coyotes. Generally either sex deer, but some buck-only areas. Minimum bow weight 40 lbs., arrow length 28", broadhead ⅞" minimum, 1-½" in length. No crossbows nor poison arrows. Compound bow okay. No dogs.

Seasons

Deer—About Oct. 21 through Nov. 12; Nov. 27 to end of year. Turkeys—Archers may use bow during gun season.

Number of bow hunters—15,359.

OREGON

Oregon State Game Commission, P. O. Box 3503, Portland, Oregon 97208

License:		
Resident	$ 5.00	
Archery tag-		
with license	2.00	
separate	5.00	
Deer tag	2.00	
Elk tag	10.00	
Nonresident	50.00	
Archery tag	2.00	
Deer tag	15.00	
Elk tag	35.00	

Bow Hunting: Only residents may apply for antelope, sheep and goat and cougar tags. Some elk areas by drawing. Minimum bow weight for elk 50 lbs. and arrow of 500 grains. Other than elk, 40 pound bow and ounce (437½ grains) arrow. Minimum barbless broadhead ⅞" width. Crossbows legal in firearms season; *not* in archery seasons. No dogs except for bears (and cougars for residents). Poison arrows not mentioned. Compound bow legal.

Seasons

Deer—About Aug. 26 to end of year depending upon county regulations. Elk—usually concurrently with deer, but generally not after Sept. 24. Jan. hunt in Rocky Mt. Elk Area. Bears (black) Aug. 1 to end of year.

Number of bow hunters—16,581.

PENNSYLVANIA

Pennsylvania Game Commission, P. O. Box 1567, Harrisburg, Pennsylvania 17120

License:		
Resident	$ 8.25	
Archery tag	2.20	
Nonresident	40.35	
Archery tag	2.20	
Anterless deer tag	3.35	

Bow Hunting: Legal for *all* game in season. No crossbows, archer's arm, or bow held, drawn or released by aid of mechanical means. No poison arrows. No stopping on highway to shoot within 25 yards of such highway. Any deer in archery seasons. Archery tag not needed in firearms season. Certain areas, bow or buckshot only. One deer, one bear a year; one turkey each spring and fall season. Compound bow okay.

Seasons

Deer—Starts first Saturday nearest Oct. 1 through Sat. nearest end of month. Opens against Dec. 26 through about two weeks in Jan. Bow legal in two-week buck firearm season opening Mon. after Thanksgiving Day. Two-day doe season with special tag, about Dec. 10 and 11. Bears—(firearms season, bow legal) One or two days season after buck season. Turkeys—Bow legal in month-long Nov. season, any turkey; again in spring gobbler season about May 5 for two weeks.

Number of bow hunters—162,000.

RHODE ISLAND

Dept. of Natural Resources, Division of Wildlife, Veterans Memorial Bldg., Providence, Rhode Island 02903

License:		
Resident	$3.25	Bow Hunting: All small game in season
Archery deer tag	5.00	and foxes permitted. Bow must be capable
Shotgun deer tag	5.00	of casting an arrow 150 paces (about
Nonresident	10.25	3 feet to a pace) and nonmechanical.
Archery deer tag	20.00	Broadheads 7/8" minimum width, con-
Shotgun deer tag	20.00	structed without rivets. Arrow must carry

name and address of person licensed. Crossbows not legal for deer; nor is poison arrow. Compound bow legal.

Seasons

Deer—Oct. 1 through Jan. 31.
   Number of bow hunters—521.

SOUTH CAROLINA

Wildlife & Marine Resources Dept., P. O. Box 167, Columbia, South Carolina 29202

License:		
Resident	$ 6.25	Bow Hunting: No special archery tag.
Nonresident	25.25	Bow legal for all game, all seasons. Two
3-day tag	12.25	turkeys a day, five the season. One deer
Game management		per day; up to five in one season. No
area permit	4.25	crossbows nor drugged arrows. No mini-

mums on bows and arrows. A number of archery hunts. Dogs in Francis Marion Area for deer and hogs. Archery hunts in Oct. and Nov. in Management Areas.

Seasons

Deer—Local variations in counties and management areas from Aug. 15 through Jan. 1. Bears—Zone One—Nov. 15 through Dec. 1. Horse Pasture Area, Oct. 30 through Nov. 4. Hogs—Legal in deer seasons. Turkeys—In season, Thanksgiving Day up to Jan. 1; Mar. 15 through April 15. By zone.

Number of bow hunters (estimated), 5,000.

SOUTH DAKOTA

Dept. of Game, Fish & Parks, State Office Bldg. No. 1, Pierre, South Dakota 57501

License: Resident
    General tag $ 1.00
    Deer—archery   8.50
    Elk   15.00
    Antelope—either
    firearm or archery   8.50
    Turkey   2.00
  Nonresident
    General tag   1.00
    Deer—archery   35.00
    Antelope—
      archery   35.00
    Turkey   5.00
    Predator   5.00
  Small game   25.00

Bow Hunting: Either big-game tag good for unprotected species. May hunt in firearms seasons with bow. Small-game tag. Minimum bow weight 40 lbs.; steel broadheads of not less than ⅞" width, 1½" long. Arrow shaft must be minimum of 24". Bow must cast arrow 125 yards. Any deer.

Seasons

Deer—Archery varies in four areas. West River: Oct. 1-Nov. 10; Dec. 1-Dec. 31. Black Hills: Oct. 1-Oct. 20; Dec. 1-Dec. 10. East River: Nov. 4-Nov. 24; Dec. 4-Dec. 31. Sand Lake: Sept. 2- Sept. 17; Dec. 4-Dec. 31. Antelope—West River only for residents—Aug. 19 through Oct. 1. Turkeys—(need general license, small game tag & turkey stamp) Oct. 21-31.
    Number of bow hunters—4,415.

TENNESSEE

Tennessee Game & Fish Commission, P. O. Box 40747, Nashville, Tennessee 37220

License: Resident $ 5.00
    Archery stamp   1.00
    Nonresident   25.00
    Archery stamp   1.00

Bow Hunting: No dogs in archery seasons. All small game and vermin legal in season. Broadhead minimum ⅞" width and barbless, arrow length at least 24". Bow must be capable of casting arrow 150 yards. No crossbows or poison arrows. Compound bow okay.

Seasons

Deer—By zone for special archery seasons: Zone I—about Oct. 9-31; Dec. 11-18. Zones II & III—about Oct. 2-31; Nov. 20-Dec. 5. Zone III—also Dec. 18-26. Bears —In season. Hogs—In season. Turkeys—In season.
    Number of bow hunters—16,360.

TEXAS

Texas Parks & Wildlife Dept., State Office Bldg., Austin, Texas 78701

License: Resident $ 3.25   Bow Hunting: No dogs. Apparently
          Nonresident   25.00   one license covers all hunting in season.
          (changes expected)   Bow must be capable of casting arrow
                                         130 yards. Broadheads not less than ⅞"
                                         in width nor more than 1½". Name and
                                         address of user must be permanently
                                         affixed to arrows. No "poisoned, drugged
                                         nor explosive arrows." No crossbows.
                                         Some counties bucks only: some allow
                                         antlerless deer by permit only.

Seasons

Deer—month of Oct. for archers. Bears—month of Oct. in certain counties for archers. Javelina—month of Oct. in certain counties for archers. Turkeys—month of Oct.

Number of bow hunters—unknown.

UTAH

Dept. of Natural Resources, Division of Wildlife Resources, 1596 West North
  Temple, Salt Lake City, Utah 84116

License: Regular   Bow Hunting: All small game in season,
            (good for deer) $ 5.00   and vermin. No dogs in archery seasons.
          Antelope permit   10.00   Guides required for bears and cougars.
          Elk permit (choice   Regular license in gunning seasons.
            of gun or bow)   15.00   No crossbows. No information on poison
          Moose permit   25.00   arrows nor compound bows.
          Sheep permit   25.00
          Turkeys   4.50
          Nonresident   75.00
          Deer   7.00
          Bears (black)   100.00
          Turkeys   20.00
          Cougar   100.00

Seasons

Deer & Elk—Special archery season concurrently in early Sept. All other game in regular firearms seasons.

Number of bow hunters—20,047.

VERMONT

Agency of Environmental Conservation, Department of Fish & Game, Roxbury, Vermont 05669

License:

Resident	$ 3.50	
Archery tag	2.00	
Nonresident	30.50	
Archery tag	5.00	

Bow Hunting: Regular hunting license permits use of bow for all game in season and vermin. Archery tag for special deer season. No crossbows nor compound bows permitted. Nothing to cover poison arrows. Broadhead must be minimum of 7/8" wide with two or more blades. Any deer in archery season. May take second deer in firearms season.

Seasons

Deer—Archery season 16 days beginning second Sat. in Oct. Bears—Firearms season Sept. 1 through Nov. 30. Turkeys—Spring gunning season by drawing about May 9-20. Residents get preference. Bow legal.

Number of bow hunters—Resident 12,407; Nonresident 8,789: Total 21,206.

VIRGINIA

Commission of Game & Inland Fisheries, P. O. Box 11104, Richmond, Virginia 23230

License: Resident

Regular state	$ 3.50	
Regular county	2.00	
Big game tag (bear, deer, turkey)	2.00	
Special stamp, big game, some counties	1.00	
Nonresident		
Regular state	15.75	
Big game (plus)	20.00	
Certain counties	5.00	

Bow Hunting: No archery tag required. Bow legal in all seasons. One deer a day; two a season in some counties; others vary according to time of season. For deer and bears, broadhead must be minimum width of 7/8"; bow must be capable of casting arrow 125 yards. No crossbow nor poison arrows. Compound bow legal. No firearms in special bow season.

Seasons

Deer—Archery, Oct. 16 through Nov. 15. Generally, firearms season Oct. 2 through Jan. 5 with local exceptions by area. Bears—Firearms season Oct. and Nov. with local exceptions; only southwest and southeast counties open. Turkeys—Firearms season in certain areas: Fall, Nov. 13 through end of year; spring gobbler, April 14-May 12.

Number of bow hunters (estimated) 25,000. (Actual survey in 1968, 22,496.)

WASHINGTON

Dept. of Game, 600 No. Capitol Way, Olympia, Washington 98501

License: Resident $ 6.50

Archery tag   5.00

Deer tag   3.00

Black bear tag   2.00

Elk tag   10.00

Sheep tag   10.00

Goat tag   10.00

Turkey tag   2.00

Nonresident   50.00

Archery tag   5.00

Deer tag   3.00

Bear tag   2.00

Elk tag   35.00

Goat tag   35.00

Turkey tag   2.00

Bow Hunting—All small game and vermin on a required nonresident license. Bow must draw 40 lbs. at 28". Broadhead minimum ⅞", sharp and without barb. No crossbows nor poison arrows. Compound bow okay. Dogs only outside deer and elk seasons when used on bears, cougars, bobcat and raccoons. Any deer in archery areas. Any elk in archery areas. Drawings. No nonresident sheep permits.

Seasons

Deer—Archery seasons in many counties varying from late Sept. through Jan. 31. Elk—Kittitas, Nov. 23-Dec. 17; Yakima, Nov. 18-26; Jefferson, Dec. 2-Jan. 31; Pacific Bow area, Nov. 13-Jan. 31. Bears—Certain areas, Sept. 23-Oct. 8; Sept. 9-Dec. 17; Oct. 14-Nov. 12. Special archery seasons on grouse, rabbits and raccoons in Bow Areas One and Two.
Number of bow hunters—10,000.

WEST VIRGINIA

Dept. of Natural Resources, Charleston, West Virginia 25305

License: Resident $ 5.00
          bow or gun
          Nonresident   30.00
          bow or gun
          Archery & fishing
          only   15.00
          Issuing fee   .25

Bow Hunting: All species of small game in season, and vermin. Except during first three days of deer firearms season. Double cutting edge required on broadhead of ¾" minimum width. No crossbows nor poison arrows. Compound bow okay. Any deer statewide except bucks only during firearms season. One deer the season. One bear. One turkey each spring and fall.

Seasons

Deer—Archery, Oct. 13 to end of year. Firearms, Nov. 19-Dec. 1. Turkeys—Firearms, Oct. 13 through Nov. 17; extended to Oct. 27 certain counties & areas. Statewide spring gobbler season, April 23-May 12. Bears—Archery, Oct. 13 to end of year. Firearms seasons in certain areas, Nov. 5-Nov. 10; Dec. 10-Dec. 22.
Number of bow hunters, about 20,000.

WISCONSIN

Dept. of Natural Resources, Box 450, Madison, Wisconsin 53701

License: Resident
Small game
and bear—
firearms
or bow $ 4.25
Deer & bears
only—(gun) 5.25
Voluntary sports-
man—all game,
fishing &
trapping 11.50
Archery—all
game 5.25
Nonresident
Small game—
gun or bow 25.50
Deer & bear—
gun 35.50
General hunting
—all game 50.50
Archery—all
game 25.50

Bow Hunting: Dogs only during 3-week special bear season in Sept. *No bow hunting* during gunning seasons for deer. Otherwise all small game in season and vermin. Minimum bow weight 30 lbs. Broadhead width minimum ⅞"; length 1½"; of well-sharpened metal. No crossbows nor poison arrows. Compound bow legal. Unlawful to possess strung or uncased bow 30 min. before or after shooting hours.

Seasons

Deer—Archery—3d Sat. in Sept. through Sun. prior to gun season opening; Sat. following close of gun season to end of year. Gun season about Nov. 18–Nov. 26. Bears—Special season for gun and bow north of highway 29, Sept. 9–Oct. 1, with dogs. Regular archery season 3d Sat. in Sept. through Sun. prior to gun season. (Note: Special archery season Oct. 28–Feb. 15 in certain areas for ringneck pheasants and Hungarian partridges.)
Number of bow hunters, 101,206 (1971).

WYOMING

Fish & Game Commission, P.O. Box 1589, Cheyenne, Wyoming 82001

License:	Resident		Nonresident
Deer	$10.00		$ 50.00
Elk & black bear	15.00	Elk & fishing	$125.00
Bighorn sheep	30.00		150.00
Mountain goat	30.00		150.00
Moose	25.00		125.00
Grizzly bear	30.00		150.00
Black bear	5.00		30.00

Antelope	10.00	50.00
Mountain lion	20.00	100.00
Small game	3.00	10.00
Archery—*for each*		
type game	3.00	5.00
Turkeys	5.00	20.00
Game birds		
(except turkeys)	5.00	25.00

Bow Hunting: Guide required on Nat'l Forests, Refuges and Parks and Wilderness Areas. Predators any time. No dogs for big game except lions. Archery tag at $5.00 for each species required even in gun season if bow is used, including small game. Deer licensed by allotment—first come, first served. Others by drawing. Minimum bow for elk, grizzly or moose, 50 lbs. capable of casting 500-grain arrow 160 yards; other big game 40 lbs. and can cast 400-grain arrow 160 yards. Crossbows—90 lb. draw weight at least 14″ with minimum bolt (arrow) of 16″. Broadhead minimum width 1″.

Seasons

General—Big-game seasons established in May each year. Special archery season for each species 10 days before firearms season.

Number of bow hunters—3,502.

THE CANADIAN PROVINCES

ALBERTA

Dept. of Lands & Forests, Edmonton, Alberta, Canada

License: *Resident		**Nonresident & ***Nonresident alien
$ 3.00	Wildlife Certificate	$ 3.00
5.00	Moose	100.00
5.00	Black bear	25.00
5.00	Elk	100.00
10.00	Trophy mountain sheep by draw . . .	200.00
3.00	Whitetail deer	50.00
5.00	Mule deer	50.00
10.00	Caribou	100.00
10.00	Grizzly bear	200.00
10.00	Cougar	75.00
3.00	Archery tag	3.00
5.00	X Non-trophy mountain sheep	None
5.00	X Camp Wainwright deer	None
10.00	X Goat	None
10.00	Antelope	None
5.00	X S416–418 Elk	None

*Resident for 12 mos. or citizen domiciled in Alberta. **Nonresident is not a resident, but has lived in Alberta for 12 mos. ***Nonresident alien is neither a resident nor a nonresident. X—By drawing. No person shall have more than three of: either elk or moose, not both; whitetailed deer, sheep, caribou or mule deer license.

Bow-Hunting: Bow must draw 40 lbs. at 28" and cast an arrow 150 yards. Broadhead barbless, with minimum width 1", or 3-bladed bodkin; arrow no less than 24". No crossbows nor poison arrows. Compound bow okay. Archery license good for all seasons and all game as well as special areas and special seasons. Small game and vermin legal on archery tag. Must wear long-sleeved garment of scarlet or blaze orange in other than archery-only zones. Guide required for big game.

Seasons

Deer, black bears, elk and sheep generally about Aug. 26–Dec. 9. Grizzly bears, April and May. Get regulations.

BRITISH COLUMBIA

Fish & Wildlife Branch, Dept. of Recreation & Conservation, Victoria, British Columbia, Canada

	B. C. Resident	Non-B. C. Resident	Non-Canadian
License:	$ 4.00	$15.00	$25.00
Tag fees to hunt		Trophy fees	Trophy fees
Grizzly bear	10.00	60.00	same as
Moose	6.00	60.00	Non-B.C.
Mountain sheep	5.00	75.00	
Caribou	5.00	60.00	
Elk	5.00	60.00	
Cougar	5.00	60.00	
Mountain goat	2.00	40.00	
Deer	1.00	25.00	
Black bear	.50	5.00	
Wolf	—	40.00	

Bow Hunting: No special archery license. Bow must be 40 lbs. at draw of 20 inches. Broadhead no less than ⅞" width. No bear baiting. Guides required for sheep, brown and grizzly bears. Basic license required. Tag fees must be paid by nonresidents to *hunt* various species. Trophy fees must be paid for *each* kill. Two deer, two black bears generally. One moose, elk, goat, sheep, grizzly bear, cougar or wolf. Some more liberal exceptions. No exploding arrows. Seasons jump all over the calendar; obtain current regulations. (mostly mid-Aug. to early Dec.) Early archery seasons on some deer and bears in restricted areas. Crossbow minimum of 120 lbs.; with broadhead minimum of ⅞", not less than 500-grain arrow, legal in *other than* archery seasons.

MANITOBA

Dept. of Tourism, Recreation & Cultural Affairs, Room 408, Norquay Bldg., Winnepeg 1, Manitoba, Canada

License: *All* hunters must possess a Wildlife Certificate at a cost of $2.25. Stamps for certificate as follows:

Resident		Nonresident
$ 6.00	Deer	$ 25.00 Canadian
		40.00 Alien
3.00	2nd deer	——
5.00	Black bear	15.00 all N.R.'s
20.00	Elk	——
16.00	Moose	30.00 Canadian
		100.00 Alien
		(includes one male
		deer, two black bears)
20.00	Caribou	100.00

Bow Hunting: Resident is person who resides in Manitoba one month; Canadian nonresident resides anywhere in Canada one month. Orange hat and white garment extending below knees must be worn in firearms season. No dogs; no Sunday hunting for big game. Bow legal in firearms season. Bow must draw 40 lbs. at 28"; barbless broadheads of minimum ⅞" width. No crossbows, poison arrows nor compound bows. Any deer in archery seasons. Any moose, caribou or elk in some areas, some seasons. Archery season only for deer. Guide not required. Small-game stamp (birds) $35.00.

Seasons

Vary for residents and nonresidents. Deer—Early archery, by area, generally late Aug. up to mid-Nov. Firearms season mid-Sept. to late Nov. by areas. Moose—Generally late Nov. to mid-Dec. Some earlier. Caribou—Mid-Sept. as late as Jan. 20. Black bears—Early to mid-Sept. to late Nov.

NEW BRUNSWICK

Department of Natural Resources, Fredericton, New Brunswick, Canada

License:	Resident		Nonresident
	$ 4.50	Any one deer and small game and vermin	$35.50
	3.00	Bear	10.00
	15.00	Moose	——

Bow Hunting: "There are no special regulations or seasons governing the use of a bow and arrow in New Brunswick. Hunters must conform with regulations in effect under the Game Act." No dogs for big game. Bear license good for two bears in spring and two in fall. Any deer in season. No cub-bears or sows with cubs. Guides generally required.

Seasons

Deer—By zones, about Oct. 23, one week in Zone 72B (eastern) and to about Nov. 18 in Zone 72A, which covers most of balance in province. Bears—April 15–June 30; Oct. and Nov.; entire province. Moose—Last 4 or 5 days in Sept. for residents only.

NEWFOUNDLAND

Dept. of Mines, Agriculture & Resources, St. John's, Newfoundland, Canada

License: Resident		Nonresident
$ 5.00	Bears	$ 15.00
15.00	Caribou	150.00—Canadian
		175.00—Alien
15.00	Moose	100.00—Canadian
		125.00—Alien
1.00	Upland game	5.00
2.00	Upland birds	5.00

Bow Hunting: No recognition of bow hunting except that it is permitted for all game if properly licensed. Bow must draw 45 lbs. and broadhead must be sharp metal not less than ⅞" in width. Crossbows permitted for small game. No poison arrows. Compound bows okay.

Seasons

None listed. Get hunting brochure.

NORTHWEST TERRITORIES

Government of the Northwest Territories, Yellowknife, N.W.T. XOE IHO, Canada

Bow hunting not legal as of Feb. 1973. Some consideration being given to bear hunting with the bow.

NOVA SCOTIA

Dept. of Lands & Forest, Wildlife Division, Box 516, Kentville, Nova Scotia, Canada

License: Resident $4.00   Nonresident $40.00
                                         (good for one deer and one bear)

Bow Hunting: Permitted. But, no equipment regulations. Special bow hunting area for residents. Moose restricted to residents. Changes expected.

Seasons

Deer—About Oct. 15–Nov. 15. Bears—Follows deer season. Moose—Residents, limited, Oct. 1–Oct. 10.

ONTARIO

Wildlife Branch, Ministry of Natural Resources, Toronto, Ontario, Canada

License: Resident

Deer & bear	$10.00
Moose & bear	15.00
Spring bear	5.25

Nonresident

Upland game & birds and wolf	$ 35.00
Deer, bear, fox, game birds, rabbit, raccoon, squirrel & wolf	40.00
As preceding, plus moose	125.00
Bear	15.00
Wolf	10.00

Bow Hunting: No equipment regulations nor special tag for bow. Crossbows and compound bows permitted. No poison arrows. Guides required in district of Rainy River. No dogs for big game. Regulations being formulated.

Seasons

Deer—Special archery—Sept. 11–29, Kenora, Rainy River, Thunder Bay; Oct. 16–31, Georgian Bay Area; Nov. 1–30, Luther Marsh hunting area. Moose—Special archery—Sept. 16–24, Northeastern area of Ontario, see regulations. Bears—All Ontario, Sept. 1 through June 30.

QUEBEC

Dept. of Tourism, Fish & Game, Quebec City, Quebec, Canada

License: Residents		Nonresidents
$ 5.25	Deer, bear, small game	$ 27.50
5.75	Anticosti Island	28.00
13.50	Moose, bear, small game	103.00
13.50	Caribou, bear, small game	103.00
5.25	Black bear	12.50
	All game (except moose and caribou)	103.00

Bow Hunting: No dogs. No special archery license. Bow weight minimum 40 lbs.; broadheads minimum width ⅞". No bow hunting on Anticosti Island. Guides needed in some parks and reserves. Crossbows permitted. Compound bow okay. Poison arrows illegal.

Seasons

Deer—Generally Oct. 28 to early Nov. Chabot Township has archery season, Oct. 14–27. Caribou—Month of Sept. Moose—By zone—earliest Sept. 16; latest Oct. 15. Black bears—May 1–July 31. Check license for other times.

SASKATCHEWAN

Tourist Branch, Dept. of Industry and Commerce, S. P. Bldg., Regina, Saskatchewan, Canada

License:	Resident	Nonresident Canadian	Alien
Deer	$ 7.00	$30.00	$ 60.00
2nd deer	6.00	—	—
Elk	15.00	—	—
Moose	—	60.00	125.00
Woodland caribou	15.00	60.00	125.00
Barren-ground caribou	10.00	—	—
Bears	5.00	—	40.00

Bow Hunting: All moose hunters must be guided. Only resident may hunt in special archery seasons. Bow must draw 40 lbs.; broadheads minimum width 1". All hunters must wear red, white or orange coveralls in gun seasons. No crossbows, no camouflage, no poison arrows, no compound bows. Name and address must be on arrows. Special elk, moose, mule deer, antelope seasons for residents only. $15.00 each tag.

Seasons

Special archery season omitted—not open to nonresidents. Deer—Either sex—generally Sept. 3 to Dec. 8. Bears—Zone 36—Sept. 3–Oct. 13; other zones, Sept. 17–Oct. 6. Moose—Either sex, Zone 36, Sept. 3–Dec. 6; Zones 34A and 35, Sept. 17–Oct. 6; Nov. 12 to Dec. 8. Woodland caribou—Generally, where available, Sept. 3–Dec. 8.

YUKON TERRITORY

Director of Game, Box 2703, Whitehorse, Yukon, Canada

License: Resident $5.00   Nonresident: $ 50.00   Canadian or British
   100.00   Alien

Kill tags:	
Black bear	5.00
Grizzly bear	65.00
Moose	25.00
Caribou	25.00
Sheep	25.00
Goat	25.00

Bow Hunting: No formal recognition, but permitted on firearms license. Guides required; usually 14-day hunt. Grouse and rabbits, coyote and wolf permitted. No special archery seasons. Crossbows permitted; compound bow okay. No poison arrows.

Seasons

Bears—black and grizzly—Aug. through Oct.; April 15–June 15. (Polar bears—Eskimos only.) Moose, caribou, sheep & goats—Aug. through Oct.

Index